# Meaningful Small Talk:

## The Shy Person's Ultimate Guide

## to Connecting with Anyone

## Dan Chang

**Meaningful Small Talk:**
**The Shy Person's Ultimate Guide to Connecting**
**with Anyone**

Printed by B.C. Allen Publishing and Tonic Books
144 N 7th St. #525
Brooklyn, NY 11249

Now taking manuscript submissions and book ideas at any stage of the process:
submissions@tonicbooks.online

Printed in the United States of America

Cover Design: Teddi Black
Interior Design: Susan Veach

ISBN: 978-0-9980299-5-5

# Contents

To my wife, Nicolette.
Thank you for always believing in me and
laughing at my jokes.

# Foreword

A GOOD WRITER knows how to simplify complex concepts and connect with readers using just a few words. The same philosophy applies to being a good conversationalist, especially when you're introverted and shy. Dan Chang is an expert at all of the above. An introvert and formerly shy guy himself, Dan takes a no-frills approach to both writing and small talk. He focuses on meaningful connection over fluff.

Though Dan and I have never met in person, we became fast online friends when he reached out to me in 2015 to talk about possible collaborations. From our first Skype chat, I could tell that Dan was the real deal. Aside from being one of the most likeable and genuine guys I know, Dan is a true leader in social skills who has helped thousands of people online and through one-on-one coaching. He is blazing trails in the world of small talk with his practical tools based on science.

His personal experiences and thousands of hours of research give Dan a valuable perspective on the challenges shy people and introverts face in conversation. He gets you. That's why his approach goes far beyond typical advice like "fake it till you make it" and "smile more."

As a card-carrying introvert myself, I have no doubt about the importance of the topic of this book. My life's work has been to help introverts build confidence and create meaningful connections. Through my website and best-selling book, I've been able to connect with millions of introverts from all over the world.

Though quiet types like us are all unique, we share many of the same challenges. Navigating small talk is definitely one of the most common and painful introvert problems. Introverts and shy people desperately want to connect, but we want to do so in a way that doesn't drive us mad with boredom or drain the life out of us.

This book provides the tools to make small talk fun, even if you're normally quiet and don't know what to say. If you'd told me ten years ago that I'd say the words "small talk" and "fun" in the same sentence, I would've laughed in your face. But when you follow Dan's science-based, introvert-friendly approach, you really can start enjoying small talk. No matter who you are, you'll get insanely clear, actionable advice to connect with others. I can tell you with confidence that this will change the way you see conversations and open new doors in your life.

—**Michaela Chung,** best-selling author of *The Irresistible Introvert* and founder of Introvert Spring

# Praise for
# *Meaningful Small Talk*

Luckily I found Dan because his material is *legit*. It's well researched, scientifically backed, and explained clearly. He does a great job taking a sea of information and packaging it into content that's easy to use and understand. And the best part—it's actionable. Even though I've been reading about social skills and psychology for many years, I still get tons of value when I ingest Dan's content. —Rob R.

Meaningful Small Talk has been a fantastic journey…I've made a lot more friends and feel a deeper connection with people. Having a detailed plan is just awesome. —Jeremiah S.

You addressed everything that I had problems with and exposed problems I didn't even know were there. It was like an epiphany and a revelation had a baby in my head. —Shawn A.

A highly compact set of fundamental principles that apply to any professional or social situation. It will show you the path, you will have to walk it. —Sid S.

I absolutely loved this... Just the 4 stages of conversation alone is worth it. If any of you is on the fence about this, please go ahead and buy it. It is a great read that will change your life.           — Diedon M.

I can feel how far I have come. Now I can make friends easily and enjoy being myself. Dan not only has great depth of knowledge about the topic, what makes him unique is he breaks down the problem and tackles each part methodically. Then he gives step by step guidance to improve. The most crucial part in any learning journey is to have the right strategy. Dan gives you that. If you follow his suggestions and practice persistently, you will become better at connecting with others and form meaningful relationships. And as a bonus it will open the door to a more successful life!           — Niloy T

This book is an amazing toolbox and will make you a better conversationalist. It's an important step in our generation's quest to make people "social" again.
                              — Paul Sanders,
                        GetTheFriendsYouWant.com

Amazing friends, a more successful career, and a fulfilling social life. Being able to connect with people via small talk will improve all areas of your life. Dan's insights are smart, fun and highly actionable. Read this book.
            — Jeff Callahan, Become More Compelling

# Introduction

WELCOME TO *Meaningful Small Talk*! If you're reading this, you want to improve your small talk skills. You'd love to easily talk to anyone, stop feeling nervous, and effortlessly connect with strangers even if you have "nothing in common."

But chances are, you can't figure out how to keep conversations going. You run out of things to say, and you're afraid of being "boring." You feel nervous, awkward, and self-conscious around new people. And talking about "lighthearted" things like the weather or traffic just seems…pointless. You zone out and can't seem to care about random chitchat.

But at the same time, you want to engage with others. You want those deep, meaningful conversations. The problem is, it's hard to get past those awkward first moments. So you end up feeling misunderstood and missing out on friends, parties, and that promotion at work.

Listen, I've been there too.

I remember struggling with shyness as a kid—OK, let's be real, as a full-grown adult too. Around new people, I would avoid conversations because I never knew what to say. My mind would go blank. I'd run out of topics really quickly. And quite honestly, I thought small talk was a waste of time. I couldn't make sense of it. I'd rather sit in silence than talk about the weather (again).

But about ten years ago, I realized this was holding me back in a huge way. I saw that people who had mastered small talk were the ones having fun, making friends, and getting promoted at work.

I remember interviewing for my dream job at a pharmaceutical company. The job was perfect. The people were nice. Things were going great. But then (cue sad trombone) they invited me to a lunch interview. Needless to say, I bombed it. They told me that I "didn't seem excited about the job."

Ouch. I was crushed.

It's not because I wasn't smart or qualified or even likable. It's because I didn't connect with them personally. I didn't know how to make small talk and connect with people! Oddly enough, I *wanted* to, and I *tried* to. But it's like something was holding me back. I just didn't know what.

So I committed myself to figuring it out.

After years of research (yes, I'm a nerd) and trial and error, I am proud to say I can start small talk with anyone without feeling nervous. I can carry on a conversation and actually enjoy it! And as a result, I've met tons of new friends and even improved my performance at work.

And no, I didn't change who I am (I'm still an introvert and relatively quiet guy). I just learned some key concepts that most people never learn. A lot of people *can't believe it* when I tell them I'm naturally shy. "What? You? Shy?"

And that's why I wrote this book.

You don't need to be the most charismatic, most interesting person. But by taking small steps, you can create big change in your life. If I can do it, so can you. There's nothing special about me. Using these concepts, you too can harness the power of small talk.

Here's the thing: avoiding small talk can handicap your life, and I want to teach you simple techniques you can use to master it. By the time you finish this book, you'll have become a small talk expert. Imagine walking into a room and being able to easily connect with anyone. In this book, I'm going to show you how, in a very simple and practical way, to do exactly that.

First, we'll go over the basics of why small talk is important, and the key mind-sets you need to succeed. And then we'll get right into the meat and potatoes. I've divided this into three main sections. First, we'll walk you through how to start talking to people. Second, you'll learn how exactly to connect with others. And third, I'll guide you through making a lasting impression.

Afterward, there's a bonus section that addresses the number one problem I hear: avoiding the awkward silences. But wait, there's more! As an *extra special* bonus, there's a "Thirty-Day Small-Talk-Mastery Plan" at the end of the book, which gives you a day-to-day, step-by-step plan to execute these principles in your real life. Sound good?

Well, I'm excited to spark a new passion in you for small talk so you can go out there and start making connections and creating opportunities in your life!

# Why Small Talk?

# Chapter 1:
# The Purpose of Small Talk

SMALL TALK GETS a bad rap. If you google "small talk," you'll see things like

- "conversations about nothing with strangers or acquaintances,"
- "light talk you don't care about," and
- "useless and boring conversation to fill awkward silences."

So it's not surprising if you find yourself zoning out during small talk—or avoiding small talk altogether. Especially if you're an introvert or deep thinker, talking about silly things doesn't make sense. Your mind starts to wander if you're not engaged within the first minute. You drift from one thought to the next, and before you know it, you're in your own little world. Listen, I get it. I'm the same way. But what if I told you that there's more to small talk than it seems?

## There Are Two Types of Intelligence

First, we need to understand the brain. Why? Our

brains have two types of intelligence. They're also known as brain networks, and this is what they're called:

- Task-positive network
- Task-negative (a.k.a. default-mode) network

The task-positive network is responsible for, well, tasks. It analyzes the mechanics of how things work, and it's really good at solving problems. We use it for things like science, math, and logical reasoning. Think of it as the analytical part of your brain. This is the typical "smart" that people think about.

On the other hand, we also have the task-negative, or default-mode, network. This allows us to connect with other people emotionally. Think of it as "social intelligence." It gives us the ability to empathize or think about how other people are feeling.

But here's the problem: during small talk, people tend to use their analytical brain, which is why they get bored, zone out, and can't think of what to say. They just can't make sense of it because the analytical brain isn't made for the job. And to make matters worse, when you use your analytical brain more, you use your social brain less.

The two networks function like a seesaw. In fact, we actually have a mechanism in our brains that won't let us use both! Your brain can't be analytical and social at the same time.[1]

---

1    Marcus E. Raichle, Ann Mary MacLeod, Abraham Z. Snyder, William J. Powers, Debra A. Gusnard, and Gordon L. Shulman, "A Default Mode of Brain Function," Proceedings of the National Academy of Sciences of the United States of America 98, no. 2 (2001): 676–82, https://doi.org/10.1073/pnas.98.2.676.

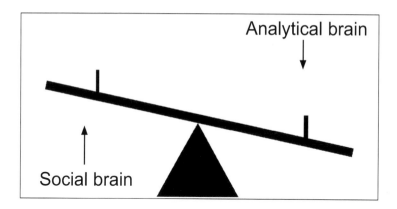

## Small Talk Uses Your Social Brain

Small talk is a social activity that requires our social brains, not our analytical brains. Therefore, the purpose is social and not analytical. In other words, *small talk is for bonding and not information.* It's not about getting stuff done; it's about getting relational. It's bonding over information. The way I like to think about it is that if big talk is the sheet music, then small talk is the musician who makes it come to life. Small talk is about communicating emotions and not so much the actual words you're using.

In general, women have higher social and emotional intelligence, whereas men are known to be more focused on analytical intelligence.[2] That's why, stereotypically, women are better with small talk, and men think it's boring and pointless. The thing is,

---

2    "New Research Shows Women Are Better at Using Soft Skills Crucial for Effective Leadership and Superior Business Performance, Finds Korn Ferry Hay Group," Korn Ferry, March 4, 2016, https://www.kornferry.com/press/new-research-shows-women-are-better-at-using-soft-skills-crucial-for-effective-leadership.

they don't realize it's a social activity that is *critical* for success.

And that's why we use it all the time. Unless you hide from humanity for the rest of your life, small talk can and will happen everywhere you go. Are there people around? Guess what? There will be small talk—at the office, business lunches, the coffee shop, weddings, and first dates. You name it. Small talk will be everywhere you go. Even with close friends and family.

- "How was work today?"
- "It's so hot out!"
- "What are your plans this weekend?"

## Small Talk Is a Human Ritual

It's everywhere we go. But why?

Think of dogs when they meet. What's the first thing they do? They start sniffing each other's butts. While this action can seem silly and pointless on the surface, something really important is actually going on here. Turns out there's more than meets the nose.

The dogs are literally sniffing out information. They can smell each other's gender, emotions, and even diet. Basically, they're smelling to figure out if they're compatible with each other. The same thing happens with humans. When we make small talk, we're "smelling" information about the other person.

- How are they feeling?
- Are they in the mood to chat?
- Are they a friendly person?
- Do I want to know them better?

In a few moments, you get thousands of bits of information that your brain takes in and processes consciously and unconsciously. But instead of butt smells, your brain picks up on words, facial expressions, and lots of little signals. It's a *ritual* that lets us get to know new people, begin bonding, and ultimately start any type of relationship, whether working, friendship, or romantic.

## The Gateway to Deep Conversation

But why bother with small talk? Can't you just jump into the deep stuff? Like "what's your biggest fear?" or "will you marry me?" Yes, technically you can. But most of the time, it will be super weird and uncomfortable. Small talk is light and easy for a reason. Dogs sniff butts, and humans use small talk. It lets us get to know each other in a low-pressure way. It's a safe way to figure out if we're compatible before any type of intense, consequential commitment is made. In a world vast with strangers, this serves a vital role in humans' social functions.

# The Door to New Relationships

By just taking that first step with small talk, you open the door to 99 percent of all relationships. In other words, if you want to make friends, 99 percent of the time, you have to start with small talk. And if you do it right, small talk can supercharge your social life. You'll make friends, enjoy parties, meet new people, and improve your performance at work.

And you'll do this using only simple small talk! Nothing complicated or super witty—just basic conversational skills. Most people don't give it the attention it deserves, but if you learn to master it, you'll be able to use it everywhere you go and connect with anyone.

## Key Points for Chapter 1

- There are two types of intelligence: social and analytical
- Small talk uses your social brain
- Small talk is a human ritual that lets us get to know other people
- Small talk is the door to new relationships

# Chapter 2:
# Small Talk Does Big Things

A SMALL THING can have a big impact. On the surface, it seems pointless. But as we discussed in chapter 1, there's more than meets the eye. In his book *The Tipping Point*, Malcolm Gladwell writes: "Look at the world around you. It may seem like an immovable, implacable place. It is not. With the slightest push— in just the right place—it can be tipped."

That's what small talk is: a slight push in just the right place. And here are some of the benefits.

## Small Talk Makes a Big Difference

Small talk opens doors to relationships. It's the path that leads to deeper stuff. Though it's sometimes hard to believe, chatting about "silly" small things really can build meaningful relationships.

Small things are important. Life is simply a collection of these small things. And these small things together grow to have exponential impact. Your body, for example, is a collection of fifty trillion small cells. Or take a piece of paper. It's only 0.05 millimeters thick. But fold it in half fifty times, and that paper will reach the height of the sun. Or did you know that a mere one-degree change in direction will put you fifty miles off course when flying from JFK to LAX? Small things can make a big difference.

With one small step, you can cause a huge chain reaction, like knocking over the first domino. When you start talking to someone, you never know what can happen. A simple "Hey, so what brings you here?" could lead into a conversation, which could lead into a friendship and then other friends and then a job opportunity, and who knows what else!

## Small Talk Broadens Your World

Albert Einstein once said, "Everybody is a genius. But if you judge a fish by its ability to climb a tree, it will live its whole life believing that it is stupid." We have a tendency to judge other people based on what we think is smart or interesting. And that's usually based on what we know, what we're good at, or what we're bad at. But each person has some sort of genius, and there's a lot you can learn from every person you meet through every small talk interaction you have, even if it's just a few minutes.

There are so many other kinds of geniuses. There are athletic geniuses, comedic geniuses, linguistic geniuses, culinary geniuses…I mean, there's pretty much a genius for anything you can think of. And even though they might not be able to engage with you about astrophysics or computer programming or whatever you're interested in, there's something that they know that you don't–someplace they've been, something they've experienced, or something they're good at.

So start thinking of small talk as opportunities to broaden your world.

Every time you meet someone new, it's an opportunity to learn something. Each person carries unique experiences from which you can learn. You expand your knowledge base by absorbing others', without having to do it for yourself. It's like CliffsNotes for real life. Through small talk, you can learn interesting things that you can turn around and use later. In many cases people will happily teach you things just because you're interested.

## Small Talk Makes You Smarter

Recent studies have shown that small talk can actually boost your mental capabilities, which were once thought to be fixed.[3] By engaging in basic small talk, people can increase their general brain function and

---

3   Oscar Ybarra, Eugene Burnstein, Piotr Winkielman, Matthew C. Keller, Melvin Manis, Emily Chan, and Joel Rodriguez, "Mental Exercising through Simple Socializing: Social Interaction Promotes General Cognitive Functioning," *Personality and Social Psychology Bulletin* 34, no. 2 (2008): 248–59, https://doi.org/10.1177/0146167207310454; Oscar Ybarra, Piotr Winkielman, Irene Yeh, Eugene Burnstein, and Liam Kavanagh, "Friends (and Sometimes Enemies) with Cognitive Benefits: What Types of Social Interactions Boost Executive Functioning?," *Social Psychological and Personality Science* 2, no. 3 (2011): 253–61, https://doi.org/10.1177/1948550610386808.

even their "executive functions," which include things like memory, attention, focus, and self-control.[4] There is a definite connection between small talk and intelligence. That's because it forces us to read people's minds and take on their perspectives. It's also fast and unpredictable. It's full of rapid exchanges back and forth and random topic changes. And by doing it as much as possible, you exercise your default mode brain and build up the ability to think on your feet.

## Small Talk Is Nice

Now that I've laid out all my arguments, here is my final point: small talk is just plain nice. It's a thoughtful way to engage other people and meet them where they feel most comfortable. Imagine if everyone could get along with others no matter when, where, or how different they may seem. If nothing else, it simply makes the world a better place.

---

### Key Points for Chapter 2

- Small talk makes a big difference
- Small talk broadens your world
- Small talk makes you smarter
- Small talk is nice

---

4    Adele Diamond, "Executive Functions," *Annual Review of Psychology* 64 (2013): 135–68, doi:10.1146/annurev-psych-113011-143750.

# Keys to Small Talk Success

# Chapter 3:
## Stop Feeling Nervous

SMALL TALK CAN be scary—especially around new people. An overwhelming feeling of self-consciousness takes over. Suddenly you're very aware of your body. Your face becomes tight, and your hands get fidgety. And worst of all, your mind goes blank. You don't know what to say. But the harder you think, the more your mind blanks.

This is the core struggle many people have connecting with others. But why does this happen? And how do we stop it? There are two main problems:

- Your social skills
- Your mind-set

For your social skills, it comes down to learning and practicing more. When you don't think you're good at something, you can get nervous. It's completely normal. That's what chapters 8 through 14 in this book will address. I'll teach you the proper steps, framework, and exercises to improve your small talk skills.

But before that, the greater issue here is your mind-set. Most people who suffer from shyness actually have decent social skills. The problem lies in the way they think—in other words, what they focus on.

## Self-Focus Is the Root of Nervousness

The key thing that causes nervousness is too much *self*-focus. During a conversation, our brain processes billions of bits of information per second. It's a whole ton of thoughts, ideas, memories, and feelings fighting for our attention. But because our attention is limited, we can only pay attention to a few things. And our brains' favorite thing to do? Focus attention on ourselves. We have a tendency to attach everything to ourselves: "Do I look cool?" "What do they think of me?"

It's human nature. But just like our natural addiction to sugar, fat, and salt, it's slowly killing us. Studies have shown that self-focus actually causes social anxiety.[5] The reason is that focusing on ourselves increases our focus on negative thoughts. Meanwhile it prevents us from being in the moment and seeing the things more positively.[6]

---

5    Darya Gaydukevych and Nancy L. Kocovski, "Effect of Self-Focused Attention on Post-event Processing in Social Anxiety," *Behaviour Research and Therapy* 50, no. 1 (2012): 47–55, https://doi.org/10.1016/j.brat.2011.10.010.

6    Jane M. Spurr and Lusia Stopa, "Self-Focused Attention in Social Phobia and Social Anxiety," *Clinical Psychology Review* 22, no. 7 (2002): 947–75, https://doi.org/10.1016/S0272-7358(02)00107-1.

# Comparing to Others Is Harmful

When it comes to self-focus, the biggest culprit is *comparing*. Specifically, comparing yourself to others. Let's break it down. Comparing is something everyone does, including me and you. We compare ourselves to people every day, and it's an automatic process that happens naturally. When we meet someone, we instantly just start comparing ourselves:

- "Am I smarter than him?"
- "Is she prettier than me?"

It happens most of the time without our even realizing it. In fact, on average, we spend 12 percent of our thoughts every day comparing. You might be thinking, "But comparing builds my confidence when I'm better than someone else!" Or maybe you're thinking, "I feel motivated when I compare myself to people who are better than me!" Yes, that may be true. You might get a quick ego boost or moment of inspiration when you compare. But ultimately, in the long run, comparing hurts us.

Studies have shown that the more people compare themselves, the more they experience negative emotions—specifically, envy and scorn.[7] Envy is when we want what someone else has. We envy people who are "better" than us. Scorn is when we feel like someone is unworthy, and we scorn people who

---

7    Susan T. Fiske, "Envy Up, Scorn Down: How Comparison Divides Us," *American Psychologist* 65, no. 8 (November 2010): 698–706, doi:10.1037/0003-066X.65.8.698.

are "worse" than us. I know this sounds harsh, but it's the truth and happens to all of us on some level.

And the thing is, these emotions end up *hurting you the most* in the long run. I've seen so many times that people who scorn others a lot end up having low confidence. And people who envy others a lot end up really nervous around "important" people. In both cases, when people compare themselves, they end up hurting themselves the most.

Comparing is also linked to other negative things like guilt, regret, defensiveness, lying, blaming others, unmet cravings, and lower job satisfaction. Perhaps the most surprising thing is that comparing actually lowers your social success more than low self-esteem.[8] I'll repeat that: *comparing lowers your social success more than having low self-esteem.*

Isn't that crazy? What's going on here?

Well, comparing creates a wall between you and others. This is because comparing makes you less capable of empathy, which affects your ability to relate with others.

Here's an example of how comparing creates a wall. Imagine you're at a party, and you see a group of people laughing and smiling. If you're comparing, you start asking yourself things like "Why aren't I having as much fun as they are?" Rather than relating to them,

---

8    Judith B. White, Ellen J. Langer, Leeat Yariv, and John C. Welch IV, "Frequent Social Comparisons and Destructive Emotions and Behaviors: The Dark Side of Social Comparisons," *Journal of Adult Development* 13, no. 1 (March 2006): 36–44, https://doi.org/10.1007/s10804-006-9005-0.

understanding them, and absorbing their positive energy, you are comparing, which has turned something positive into a negative thing. Pretty bizarre, right? Here's the bottom line: *comparing divides people, and it hurts your chances of making friends.*

When you stop comparing, it's easier to approach people and have conversations. The reason this works is that you shift the focus off yourself. Studies have shown that focusing on yourself increases nervousness. And that's because you have easier access to your negative thoughts and feelings. You start asking yourself things like "Do I sound awkward?" and "Am I bothering them?"

Not only that, but too much self-focus prevents you from being in the moment. According to Jessica Dore, writing for Vice's *Tonic* blog, "as more of our attention turns inward, the more self-conscious we feel. That takes up a lot of our bandwidth, and then we have very little left over for actually paying attention."[9]

And with small talk, learning to shift the focus off yourself is *key* because the less familiar you are with the person and the more trivial the topic (i.e., small talk), the more likely you are to rate the conversation based on your own performance. In other words, during small talk, we naturally focus on ourselves. And if it goes badly, we tend to blame it on ourselves.

---

9    Jessica Dore, "This Is Why Small Talk Makes Some People So Anxious," *Tonic* (blog), *Vice*, June 19, 2018 (2:56 p.m.), https://tonic. vice.com/en_us/article/mbknqv/this-is-why-small-talk-makes-some-people-so-anxious.

So in order to overcome nervousness with small talk, we have to learn to shift the focus off ourselves.

## Replace Comparing with Equalizing

OK, now how do you actually do it? If you've ever tried to stop a bad habit, you know it's really hard. The more you try *not* to do something...the more you end up doing it. So instead of simply telling yourself to stop comparing, you have to *replace* it with new behavior.

Here's a simple method you can use called "equalizing." The great thing is that this is a mental exercise that can be done in your mind, and once you test it out for yourself, you'll see that it really helps get rid of a lot of the nervousness that's holding you back.

Anytime you notice yourself thinking someone is better or worse than you, make up something in your mind that's the opposite. Seriously, make up something. It doesn't even matter if it's true. For example, maybe they look like a slob...but they're incredibly generous. Maybe they're rich...but incredibly insecure.

The point is, you're balancing out any comparing that you do and conditioning your brain to bounce the other way when you start to feel inferior or superior to other people. You're neutralizing the negative effects of comparing and, at the same time, taking the focus off yourself. For more details on how to get started go to Day Four of the Thirty-Day Small-Talk-Mastery Plan.

# Key Points for Chapter 3

- Self-focus is the root of nervousness
- Comparing yourself to others is harmful
- Replace comparing with equalizing

# Chapter 4:
# Build True Confidence

WHEN PEOPLE TALK about confidence, they're usually (whether they realize it or not) referring to "social confidence." The ability to walk into a room and not be nervous. To be comfortable in their own skin. To talk naturally, flowing smoothly from one topic to the next, and to make friends effortlessly. At its core, social confidence is *knowing* that you can talk to anyone and build a connection.

It's what we all want, right? That's why thousands of books have been written about it and why every woman and man says they're attracted to (you guessed it) "confidence."

So how do we find this elusive so-called confidence? Search online, and you'll find some terrible advice: "Look in the mirror and smile!" "Strike confident poses!" "Think positive!" If only it were that easy.

Listen, I'm all for techniques and shortcuts. Heck, that's what this book is for. But the truth is, so much of the advice out there is bad. There's little evidence —

and in fact conflicting evidence—that techniques like these work for shy people.

Enough is enough.

Let's stand conventional wisdom on its head and get to the real problem, starting first with common mistakes you should avoid.

## Mistake #1: Trying to *Feel* Confident

Confidence is not an emotion that you feel. *It's a state of mind.* Most people don't realize this, so they chase confidence as a good feeling and end up doing this:

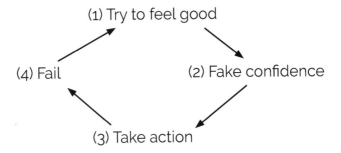

(1) Try to feel good

(4) Fail

(2) Fake confidence

(3) Take action

The result is a vicious cycle driven by *feelings*. For example, let's say you're getting ready for a party. You know important people will be there, so you start to *feel* nervous. Naturally, you try to get rid of those bad *feelings* and focus on good, happy *feelings*. In other words, you look for *feelings* of confidence. This creates what I call "fake confidence" because it's all based on *feelings*. Inevitably, your confident *feelings* falter as you stumble your way through conversations. Each stutter chips away at your "confidence," and you go home *feeling* like a failure. So naturally you try to make yourself feel better again. You're focused on *feeling* more confident, even when you're not actually confident.

Does that sound familiar?

That's why popular advice like "power posing" doesn't work. The idea is to feel confident by mimicking confident body language. Sounds like a good idea. There's even a fancy scientific explanation about hormones and cortisol levels. But it turns out this is bad advice that actually hurts people. In fact, if you have low confidence, it has the opposite effect![10] Trying to *feel* confident doesn't work. According to Joseph Cesario, an associate professor of psychology at Michigan State University, "feeling powerful may feel good, but on its own does not translate into powerful or effective behaviors."[11]

Chasing feelings is like eating junk food before a marathon. It feels good at first, but there's no real nutrition to sustain you. And ultimately it burns you out, leading to failure. True confidence doesn't waver because *it's a way of thinking, not a feeling.*

---

10  Jay Van Bavel, "The Dark Side of Power Posing: Cape or Kryptonite?," *Mind Guest Blog, Scientific American,* November 21, 2013, https://blogs.scientificamerican.com/mind-guest-blog/the-dark-side-of-power-posing-cape-or-kryptonite/.

11  Joseph Cesario and Andy Henion, "Eleven New Studies Suggest 'Power Poses' Don't Work," *MSUToday,* September 10, 2017, https://msutoday.msu.edu/news/2017/eleven-new-studies-suggest-power-poses-dont-work/.

# Mistake #2:
# Focusing on Positive Affirmations

This is a really popular technique taught by the biggest gurus in self-help. Look yourself in the mirror and tell yourself you're awesome. Do this five times a day, and make sure to smile. The idea is that if you repeat positive things to yourself over and over, then your mind will start to believe it.

Just like power posing, studies have shown that positive self-affirmation can actually make people with low self-esteem feel worse. In other words, it backfires on the people who need it most.[12] How insane is that!

If deep down inside, you believe you're an "awkward loser," no amount of positive affirmations will change that. In fact, repeating positive affirmations will create an inner battle. Let's say you're terrible at cooking. Every time you repeat "I'm a great cook!" your subconscious will immediately respond with "That's not true!" It's the same cringe you feel when you receive a compliment that isn't true. It's called cognitive dissonance, and our brains don't like it.

Your subconscious brain can't be fooled that easily. It won't work if these positive affirmations are the opposite of deep-rooted beliefs. You'll end up swing-

---

12    Joanne V. Wood, W. Q. Elaine Perunovic, and John W. Lee, "Positive Self-Statements: Power for Some, Peril for Others," *Psychological Science* 20, no. 7 (2009): 860–66, https://doi.org/10.1111/j.1467-9280.2009.02370.x.

ing back and forth between extreme thoughts, from "I'm awesome! I can do this!" to "I'm a failure. I suck." The result is that you will end up feeling worse than when you started.

## Mistake #3: Relying on Looks and Achievements

Logically this makes sense. Look more attractive? Get more confidence. Make more money? Get more confidence. This is how many people try to build their confidence, by pursuing looks and achievement. "Of course people will like me if I'm rich, beautiful, and successful, right?"

The problem is that your looks and achievements are conditional. In other words, they're not lasting. And even if you're unbelievably attractive or great at something, there's always someone who's better and more attractive than you. Or what if you suddenly lose it all? What happens after that? Do you lose all your confidence?

You'll never become socially confident by focusing on becoming better than others. There will always be someone who's better than you. And even if you achieve a lot and become awesome, if you're perfectly honest with yourself, you'll still be weak in many areas of your life. It's a tough battle to fight.

# Focus on Others, Not How You Feel

Social confidence is *knowing* you can talk to anyone and build a connection.

And here's the truth. It doesn't come from what you feel, look, or achieve. It doesn't come from what others think of you, or even what you think of yourself. It's a mind-set—and knowing where to focus.

*True social confidence comes from focusing on others, not yourself.*

When you worry about how you look or feel, you're self-focused and can't pay attention to others. Because your attention is turned inward, you become less socially engaged. As we talked about in chapter 3, when we focus too much on ourselves (what we say, how people perceive us, how interesting we are), this increases our anxiety and lowers our confidence. But if you shift your focus onto others, you'll be more perceptive and far more socially confident.

Remember, a key reason you lack confidence is because you doubt yourself. You filter things because you don't want to make a mistake or say something stupid. You worry what others might think. All of this is caused by too much self-focus.

Instead, even though it seems counterintuitive, you must focus less on yourself—and focus more on others. This is the little-known secret to confidence that nobody talks about. If you want to love yourself more, begin by thinking of yourself less. Just like there's incredible pleasure when you watch movies and escape into other worlds, there's incredible freedom when you immerse yourself in the lives of others instead of dwelling on your own issues.

When you focus on others, that's when you *become* confident (not just feel confident). This completely changes the game. It's crazy. You get out of your head and stop living inside your thoughts. No longer are you searching for ways to boost your ego or to stop those nervous feelings. It just starts to happen. It's crazy how this works.

I'm not saying don't think highly of yourself. Of course you're special, amazing, and beautiful—nothing wrong with telling yourself that. But if you want to become truly confident and *know* deep down that you can connect with others, the only way is to focus on others.

## Focus on Others by Serving Them

Now we have to be careful. When I say focus on others, I don't mean that you should focus on how they treat *you* or react to *you* or what they're thinking about *you*. That just ends up being a sneaky, twisted way of thinking about ourselves.

Therefore, the best thing is to focus on others by *serving them*. A study from British Columbia found that "being busy with acts of kindness"[13] can help people reduce their social anxiety. Focusing on serving others countered the participants' fears of

---

13    https://link.springer.com/article/10.1007/s11031-015-9499-5

rejection, lowered their levels of stress and anxiety, and, at the same time, made room for more positive thoughts and observations. In the end, participants in the study actually found that people responded more positively to them than they expected.

By serving others, they ended up building their own confidence.

---

## Key Points for Chapter 4

- Mistake #1 is trying to feel confident
- Mistake #2 is focusing on positive affirmations
- Mistake #3 is relying on looks and achievements
- Focus on others, not how you feel
- Focus on others by serving them

# Chapter 5:
# Become a "Natural"

SO WHEN'S THE last time you *wanted* to say something but *didn't*? Maybe you doubted yourself, or maybe you felt embarrassed, so you stayed silent. If you're shy, you know exactly what I'm talking about.

Meanwhile, some people seem to be "naturals." They weave in and out of topics, gliding around like ballerinas on ice. They have the ability to talk to anyone about anything—even strangers (when most people freak out). They make it look so darn easy.

## Think Out Loud

If you watch "naturals," you'll notice they don't hesitate. They don't doubt themselves, they speak genuinely, and they seem to have a great time. Are they just born with it? Sure, maybe. But not all of them. Many "naturals" admit to being quiet and awkward kids. Social skills (like anything else) can be practiced and learned.

So what's their secret? What do they do differently? *They think out loud.* This means they don't overprocess and overanalyze things inside their head *before* they say it. Instead, they take their internal thoughts and bring them to the outside world—raw and uncut.

The reason naturals seem like they don't think twice is that...they don't! Their analytical brain doesn't get in the way of their social brain.

With small talk, there's no time for you to process, and ponder before you speak. That's not how conversations work. They're too random and spontaneous. When you dwell inside your head, looking for something to say, that's exactly when you freeze up. The more you think, the more your mind blanks. You get stuck inside while the conversation moves forward without you. Think about it: it's impossible to have two conversations at the same time—talking to yourself *and* talking to someone else.

Instead, speak your true thoughts—as much as you can. If you think it, then speak it. The more you do this, the more harmony you'll feel inside and out. People will feel it too, and they will connect with you authentically. You might be thinking, "But I don't have any thoughts to share." And that's simply not true. I'm willing to bet you have plenty of thoughts. You're just so used to filtering that you've convinced yourself that none of them is worth saying out loud.

# You Probably Filter Yourself Too Much

We all have a filter inside our minds. Much like this coffee maker:

The stuff that goes in—the grounds and water—is our thoughts. And the stuff that comes out—the coffee—is our words. When a thought enters our mind, the filter decides, "Yes, that's OK to say" or "No, don't say it." Everyone does this on some level. And having a filter is good because it prevents us from saying things that get us into trouble. It's trying to protect us.

But here's the rub: like an overprotective parent, shy people have *overactive* filters. And because of that, nothing gets through. It's like having a coffee filter that makes no coffee. They filter too many thoughts.

What about you? Do you filter too many of your thoughts? Let's take a moment to evaluate your personal filter. The scale below ranges from 0 to 10, where 0 is obnoxious and 10 is silent.

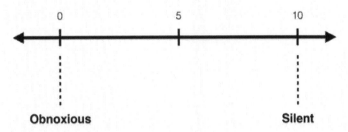

**Your Filter Scale**

If you're shy and tend to filter what you say, you'll land more toward the right. If you're very vocal and don't really filter your thoughts, you'll fall more toward the left. Now take a moment to think. Where do you fall on this scale?

- **0–1:** You say everything that comes to mind, even if it hurts others and yourself.

- **2–4:** You say most of your thoughts but will hold back if a thought is extremely inappropriate.

- **5:** You say a good portion of your thoughts, but many are filtered

- **6–7**: You say about half of your thoughts and filter the rest.

- **8–10:** You have a hard time speaking up on a daily basis, even when you're supposed to.

If you fall toward the right, at 8 through 10, this chapter is especially important for you. Most likely your filter is too strong.

# Filtering Keeps You Locked in Jail

Brad Blanton, in his book *Radical Honesty*, has this to say about filtering: "Withholding from people, not telling them about how we feel or think, keeps us locked in jail. The longer we remain in that jail the quicker we decline."

Not speaking your mind (a.k.a. filtering yourself) keeps you locked in jail. And what happens in the long run is that you filter yourself so much that you don't trust what you have to say anymore. These are some real quotes from real people:

- "Over the years, I've become so dishonest with myself that I no longer feel like I exist."
- "I feel like a ghost."

Every time you feel like you *should* say something and then *don't*, a part of you gets lost inside. And this is the real danger of filtering. You lose your authentic voice that is uniquely yours.

And the social danger is huge too. Filtering keeps you from connecting with people. That's because filtering yourself is not authentic. You don't show people the true you, and therefore people will never get to know the true you. In order to connect, people need to feel like you're being authentic. And if you filter yourself, you communicate on a subconscious level that you have something to hide. After all, if you had nothing to hide, why would you need to filter yourself?

## You Can't Mess Up

Not filtering yourself can sound scary. But think of it this way. If you're being authentic and truly say what's on your mind, you can't mess up. You have *tons* of thoughts, hobbies, and life opinions to share. And like we've said before, it's just that you process and filter them out.

Take kids, for example. One reason why people love kids is because they're *so honest*. They are being themselves 100 percent, and therefore they can't mess up. We love the silly things they say. We even love the grumpy ones.

Let's channel that same mind-set with small talk. Sure, you might say some things that aren't that funny or are maybe a little awkward, but it's natural—and completely normal. Even if you do offend someone, it's as simple as apologizing or clarifying what you meant. And people will appreciate your honesty. To have a great conversation, you must be you. It needs to be natural. The minute you're not you, it's going to be weird, both for you and the other person.

# Let Go of the Perfect Thing to Say

I've found that people who struggle with speaking up also struggle with perfectionism. They feel like they need to prepare the perfect thing to say in their head before they say it. They don't want to be boring or cliché, so they think and think and end up paralyzing themselves. For example, they'll meet someone new and think they need to say something that's not corny or cliché. And ultimately, they end up not saying anything at all.

But good news, friend: there is no perfect thing to say. Read that again and say it aloud. *There is no perfect thing to say.* Just look around. In general, people just want to be around their friends and have a good time talking about lighthearted things. Go to a mall and walk around for an hour. Listen to what people say. They talk about some pretty silly stuff.

You won't have the perfect thing to say. And that's OK. Say it anyway. Something is better than nothing. Keep things simple and follow the basics. You don't need to reinvent the wheel. I've seen that a lot of charismatic people with lots of friends don't always say the perfect thing. In fact, they "mess up" quite a lot. They just have relaxed, fun conversations about silly things. Let go of the perfect thing to say.

# Trust Your Social Brain

I know it's scary not to think about something before

you say it, but just trust your social brain. It will come up with something in the moment—and sometimes even clever and funny things. With some practice, you'll surprise yourself. If you really focus on the other person, and really listen, your brain will take care of the rest.

And when you're focused on bringing others joy and kindness, the perfectionism dissolves. You'll speak more freely, people will respond to you, and you'll gain more trust in yourself. Just let go and have some faith.

Want to get practical? Go do the exercise on Day Five in the "Thirty-Day Small-Talk-Mastery Plan."

---

## Key Points for Chapter 5

- Think out loud
- You probably filter yourself too much
- Filtering keeps you locked in jail
- You can't mess up
- Let go of the perfect thing to say
- Trust your social brain

# Step One: Starting Small Talk

# Chapter 6:
# Easiest Way to
# Start Talking to Anyone

STARTING CONVERSATIONS CAN be scary, especially with strangers. So here's what most people do:

- They try to be impressive
- They try to be clever
- They prepare impressive stories
- They use powerful body language

But these don't actually help you connect with people. And it can be extremely paralyzing, especially if you're shy. You end up getting stuck in your head and talking to nobody.

*So what does that mean?*

Instead of focusing on yourself, focus all your attention on the other person. If you focus on yourself, you'll get nervous. And if you focus on information, the interaction will be over quickly. For example, let's say you start a conversation by asking for the time:

You.        Hey, do you know what time it is?
STRANGER. Eleven fifteen.
You.        Great—thanks!
STRANGER. No problem. (*Turns away.*)

It becomes transactional rather than relational. And it's really hard to get a conversation going like that. So when you start, the key is to focus on the person and not on yourself or the information. I know that sounds contradictory, but remember, it's about getting to know the other person, so don't put pressure on yourself or the subject matter.

Now what exactly do you say?

## Cliché Is OK

You aren't going to say anything earth-shattering. And that's OK.

When you start conversations, cliché is OK. Actually, cliché is what you want to aim for. This keeps things simple. Boring and predictable is actually a good thing.

We often try to think of clever things to say, but this paralyzes us. That's because our brains dismiss most of our ideas. We think, "That's so unoriginal; nobody wants to hear that." But most of the time, that's not true! The big thing I want you to understand is that it's supposed to be cliché.

Cliché is OK. There's comfort in typical questions. Starting with something unoriginal makes people more comfortable. The most important thing, which isn't cliché at all, is that you approach the person and talk to them. That alone sets you apart from 99 percent of the people out there.

Here are some examples of how I've started some conversations using some cliché stuff:

- There was a woman on the train wearing a Dropbox T-shirt, so I asked her, "Do you use Dropbox?" We talked for fifteen minutes, and she gave me her business card.

- Another time I saw a guy in the city with a tattoo, and I said, "I like your tattoo." We talked for a half hour and exchanged phone numbers.

- One time, I was on the plane, flying to Chicago, and I turned to the person next to me and asked, "You traveling for business?" We ended up talking for the entire flight, we exchanged numbers, and he actually just texted me last night.

As you can see, I didn't have to be witty or unique. I simply focused on the other person and started these conversations with cliché topics.

And here are the four easiest ways you can start talking with anyone. They are really easy. And the great thing is, they're natural, won't weird people out, and minimize your chances of getting rejected. Just stick with these, and you'll do great.

# Observation of a Shared Experience

Let's start with the easiest one: an observation of a shared experience.

What you're going to do is comment on something that you're both experiencing. Simple, right? What this does is create an instant bond. Just the fact that you're both experiencing something at the same time gives you something in common.

People are always on the lookout for others similar to themselves. And this is an easy way to do that. Here are some simple examples:

- "Wow, this place is packed."
- "Is it just me, or is it insanely hot in here?"
- "Did you see that?"

Just pointing out stuff in the shared environment is a great way to start a conversation.

# Compliment plus Question

The next one is fun: a compliment plus a question, with a special emphasis on the question. While most people like compliments, they won't know how to respond, so a question helps remove the awkwardness and drive the conversation forward.

The best thing is to compliment something that they're wearing or carrying. The reason this works is that it's something personal, but it's not too personal.

They've obviously put in some thought because they chose to wear it. But at the same time, it's not overly personal and intrusive, like asking about their... medical history or something.

Some examples ar:e

- "I like your hat—what's that called?" and
- "Hey, cool shirt—where'd you get it?"

This really works. I've done it so many times, and it's amazing. It doesn't have to be complicated.

## Offer Help

Third, you can offer someone help. People who need help are literally hoping someone will approach them. They're in need. So what you're going to do is find these people. For example, you can look for people who

- look lost and need directions,
- look bored, or
- are carrying something heavy.

Once you find someone, simply help them!

What this does is leverage the rule of reciprocity. It's the universal tendency for people to feel compelled to repay a kind deed or act of generosity. In other words, if you help someone, they're going be much nicer to you and almost feel a *need* to repay you. This is a great time to start a conversation with people, after you've helped them and they feel indebted to you.

Now it's important that we don't expect anything in return. If they're busy or the timing isn't right, it's OK. You've improved their day and made the world a nicer place.

## Ask Someone Their Opinion

This one is my absolute favorite: ask someone for their opinion. I love this one because it works every time; it's amazing. Most people will say yes if you ask them for an opinion because it's easy and it's non-threatening. And it also works great because it makes them feel valued. You're basically saying, "Hey, I care about what you think. Would you mind helping me out?" Very few people will say no.

What I like to do is ask for someone's opinion while I'm shopping. Let's say I'm looking at clothes. I'll say, "Excuse me. I could really use a female opinion. Which one of these shirts do you think looks better on me?" I've gotten some really interesting responses and started some really fun conversations. And it's really, really easy to do.

Here are some more examples you can use at a store or restaurant:

- "Do you know what's good here?"
- "Have you tried this? Is it good?"
- "Can you help me decide which one to get?"

# Key Points for Chapter 6

- Cliché is OK
- Make an observation of a shared experience
- Give a compliment and ask a question
- Offer someone help
- Ask someone their opinion

# Chapter 7:
# The Key Principle of Great Small Talk

AFTER YOU'VE STARTED a conversation, it's important to understand the key principle of small talk. You can start by thinking of yourself as a talk show host. Close your eyes and take a moment to imagine it...*Late Night with [Your Name]*! Hear the band; see the lights. The audience is cheering. Your first guest walks out and sits down. Here we go. It's time for small talk.

What do you do?

What do you say?

Most importantly, how do you want your guest to *feel*?

Take a moment to think about some great talk show hosts. Or even go search YouTube for some Jimmy Fallon, Craig Ferguson, or Ellen DeGeneres interviews and watch the first minute or so. They are all experts at small talk. In fact, they are paid millions of dollars to make small talk professionally. What do they all have in common? How do they make their guests *feel*?

## Small Talk Creates Comfort

A talk show host helps their guest feel *comfortable*. That's arguably their main job. In order for the guest to talk (which is kind of important for a *talk* show), they have to feel comfortable. That's why the hosts use small talk. It's a tool to masterfully get a sense of the guest's mood and their personality and to make them comfortable.

Small talk *creates comfort*. This is the fundamental principle, or "rule," of small talk. So during small talk, keep this in mind. And think of yourself as the talk show host. It's your job to create comfort. It's up to you to take control and assume that responsibility. In order for people to enjoy your company, you need to make it easy for them. And that's right: *comfortable*.

## Make People Feel Good

Let's get practical. How exactly do you create comfort?

The first and easiest way is to make people *feel good*. And the best way to make them feel good is to get them to talk about themselves. This is also known as "self-disclosure." And self-disclosure makes people feel good. A study from Harvard found that self-disclosure actually triggers the brain's mesolimbic dopamine system in the same way that sex, cocaine, and good food do.[14] In other words, it feels pretty dang good.

And the best way to get people to talk about themselves is to be curious and ask questions. We'll talk more about that in chapter 8.

Another simple thing you can do to make people feel good is to use the word *you* as much as possible. The word *you* peaks a person's attention and is similar to hearing their own name—which everyone loves the sound of. So try replacing *I* with *you* as much as you can. Even if you're talking about yourself, use *you* more, and it works wonders.

Here's a quick example.

Imagine you're talking about your day: "So *I* woke up today at 5:00 and had one of those peaceful mornings all to myself where *I* got to sit at the table and just be alone with *my* thoughts. *I* don't get those days very often."

OK, not bad, right?

But watch what happens when you swap out all the *I*s with *you*s: "So I woke up today at 5:00 and had one of those peaceful mornings all to *you*rself where *you* get to sit at the table and just be alone with *you*r thoughts. *You* don't get those days very often."

See the difference that makes?

---

14    Diana I. Tamir and Jason P. Mitchell, "Disclosing Information about the Self Is Intrinsically Rewarding," *Proceedings of the National Academy of Sciences of the United States of America* 109, no. 21 (2012): 8038–43, doi:10.1073/pnas.1202129109.

Suddenly the story becomes much more relatable and comfortable to listen to.

## Be Nonthreatening

Another key to making people comfortable is to be nonthreatening. As a shy person; it's weird to think that I might be threatening. But the thing is, shyness can look threatening on the surface because it's confused with arrogance and other negative attitudes. It's crazy, I know, so what can we do about it?

Here's a really simple idea: *talk to them like a child.*

Basically, talk to them like you would talk to a child. This is from Leil Lowndes, and, as ridiculous as it sounds, it really works. If you notice, most people change the way they talk when they're around kids. Their voice gets higher, they talk more enthusiastically, and their body language becomes more inviting. And that's the energy we want to channel when we make small talk! The point here is, don't be afraid to express your emotions. You're not actually using baby talk. You're just talking naturally with a bit more animation.

You can also use *artificial time constraints.*

When you start a conversation with a stranger, let them know that there's an end in sight. In other words, it'll be fast. People don't like feeling trapped, so you start by saying something like "Hey, I'm on my way out, but before I left I wanted to ask you something..." This takes off the pressure, and it's a lot easier for both of you to be in the moment and enjoy the conversation—because, hey, it's ending soon, right?

The great thing about this is that people end up getting so comfortable that it often leads to full-blown conversations. Last week I started talking to a guy using this, expecting one or two minutes, and we ended up talking for a half hour!

## Be Agreeable

And the final way to create comfort is to be agreeable. Small talk is a time for having fun together. So when people talk to you about the weather or traffic or some random thing, they're not really talking about the weather or traffic or that random thing. They're trying to find a way to connect with you.

So don't contradict what they say.

And don't try to be smarter than them.

Just be agreeable. (There's always time for deep discussions later.)

There's a guy I know who loves to say, "Well, I don't know about that," after I say something. It's like he's trying to correct me or beat me. And guess what? I hate talking to him—and so does everyone else.

It's fine to have different opinions, but you can disagree with someone and still be agreeable.

There's a rule from improv comedy called the "yes, and" rule, and it's great for creating comfort. The general rule here is to accept what the other person says

by saying yes and then build upon it with "and."
Think of it like building the layers of a cake. They
add a layer; then you add a layer.

For example, if someone says, "I love babies;
they're so cute," you can say, "Yes, *and* they smell so
good too!" By saying "yes," you're communicating to
them, "I hear you, and I understand you." And then
you build on their idea and move the conversation
forward. It's amazing. Even if you disagree, you can
use the "yes, and" rule. By simply starting your sentences with "yes," you're able to create comfort while
also sharing your opinion.

So remember: the key principle (or ground rule)
of small talk is to create comfort. Small talk is more
than the words you're saying. It's about bonding and
emotions, not the actual exchange. People will forget
what you *say*, but they will always remember how
you make them *feel*. So it's your job to make them feel
comfortable.

---

## Key Points for Chapter 7

- Small talk is to create comfort
- Make people feel good
- Be nonthreatening
- Be agreeable

# Step Two: How to Connect

# Chapter 8:
# Turn on Detective Mode

GET EXCITED! IN this chapter, you're going to learn how to connect. I love this because this is where we start moving small talk into the meaningful. And by doing this, you will make people feel good while at the same time making yourself less nervous.

## We Think about Ourselves a Lot

As people, we think about ourselves a lot. It's natural. First thing in the morning, look in the mirror and think, "How do I look? How do I feel? What do I want to eat? What do I want to do today?" And during small talk, it's the same thing: "How do I sound? Do they like me?"

But the problem is, with small talk, the more we focus on ourselves, the less we connect. In this chapter, we're going to flip that. Instead of focusing on ourselves, we're going to focus all our attention on the other person.

# Become a Detective

Instead of asking, "How am I doing?" ask your-self, "How are *they* doing?" What's going on in *their* world? Become a detective who really wants to understand other people. I love this quote from Steven Moffat, writer and producer of *Doctor Who* and *Sherlock*; when asked about overcoming his shyness, he said, "I've come to understand that charm isn't being funny. Charm is finding other people funny."

The most charming people are those that are interested in others. By focusing on others, you can get them to open up and talk about themselves. As discussed in chapter 7, this is called self-disclosure, and it makes people feel good. When we talk about ourselves, those are the conversations we enjoy most. That's because when we share and the other person listens, we start building a connection. Self-disclosure usually looks something like this.

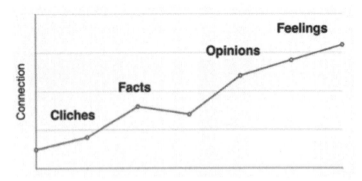

As you move along from left to right, you get deeper and start connecting. Having conversations like this is how you connect. And this will serve as the framework for every conversation: Clichés → Facts → Opinions → Feelings. Let's clarify what each of these mean.

| Clichés | Facts | Opinions | Feelings |
|---------|-------|----------|----------|
| "How are you?" "How's it going?" "Nice weather today." | Weather Traffic Current events Weekend plans | "I like..." "I don't like..." "I prefer..." | "I'm glad..." "I'm excited..." "I'm nervous about..." |

**Clichés** are common everyday phrases and topics that people use for small talk. Some examples include "How are you?" or "Nice weather today." These are harmless ways to start a conversation. You learned all about clichés in chapter 6.

**Facts** are information that don't get too personal—for example, talking about the weather, current events, or weekend plans. This is really neutral stuff and, in my opinion, really boring stuff. People don't really care about basic details like names, dates, numbers, and everyday events. They care about what makes you unique! So that's why we want to focus on the transition from facts to opinions.

**Opinions** are where the magic starts to happen. Opinions are what make people unique. This is where you start to uncover the true person. Examples of opinions are things like "I like," "I don't like," and "I prefer."

Finally, **feelings** are about specific emotions—so,

for example, "I'm glad," "I'm excited," or "I'm nervous about."

## Uncover Opinions and Feelings

Most people get stuck at clichés and facts, like talking about the weather or traffic. But by doing that, they're basically *hoping* they connect. The truth is, unless you're deepening your conversations and moving along this line, you're not connecting. Specifically, you want to focus on moving from facts to opinions. In other words, move from *what* to *why*. Instead of *"Where* do you live?" think *"Why* do you live there?"

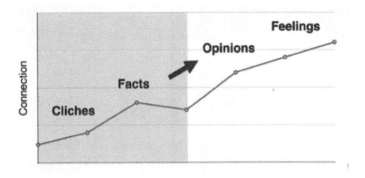

Specific questions will get specific answers and move you away from clichés and facts into the deeper stuff. This helps open up even reserved people because they see that you actually care.

Really focus on the transition from facts to opinions (the arrow above). You need to move the conversation forward and deepen it by uncovering opinions and feelings. That's where connection happens, where you move from superficial to meaningful. Here's an example of how to do it step by step:

1.  Instead of asking the generic "How are you?" ask something just a little more specific, like "How's your day going so far?"

2.  From there, continue asking specific questions to really understand their day. Think of this as gathering facts.

    a.  "What's going well? What isn't?"

    b.  "Doing anything fun?"

    c.  "Any plans for tonight?"

3.  From there, the conversation can go into a whole range of topics. I find people end up talking a lot about their jobs or their families.

4.  In any case, continue asking questions that really draw on their opinions and feelings.

    a.  "Do you enjoy that?"

    b.  "Are you excited?"

    c.  "What's that like? It must feel great."

    d.  "Is that your favorite thing to do?"

    e.  "Are you attracted to me?" (*wink*) (just kidding, don't do that!)

## Be Curious, and Ask What Comes to Mind

Like I said, most people get stuck at clichés and facts because they don't really care, which is why small talk usually sucks. But you're going to be different. You're going to actually care. How? Be curious, and ask what comes to mind. For a shy person, questions are a great tool to use.

Watch any great conversationalist, and they ask tons of questions. Questions are powerful. What usually makes questions boring is asking boring questions. Meaningful questions, however, make meaningful small talk.

The key is to be curious and ask what comes to mind. So let's say, for example, someone is talking about a trip to Italy. What are the questions that come into your mind? Maybe some of these:

- "What's it like there?"
- "Who did you go with?"
- "Did you buy anything?"
- "Why did you choose Italy?"
- "How was the food?"

Just be curious, and don't filter yourself. If you get stuck, here are some questions you can always fall back on:

- "How did you...?"
- "Why did you...?"
- "What was that like?"

These are great because they start to uncover opinions and emotions and move you along that line. And here's an easy go-to question you can use anytime: "Do you like...?"

It's really simple, but it works great. Use it as a shortcut that cuts right to opinions. You'll be surprised what comes out of it. Great conversationalists use this question all the time. Just watch how often my man Craig Ferguson uses it: www.thefriendformula.com/doyoulike.

## In a Nutshell

In summary, remember to focus on others. Then uncover opinions and feelings. The best way to do this is by being curious and asking what comes to mind. In case it's still not clear, here's a real-life example from one of my students. Here's how he used detective mode to connect. Afterward, he told me, "I could feel the conversation being built on clichés, facts, opinions, feelings. I am good at connecting. Now I am doing it in a structured way."

| The Conversation | The Phase |
|---|---|
| We started the conversation about what we did yesterday. They did meditation. | CLICHÉS |

↓

| It built to what they normally do on the weekend. They have a two-year-old daughter. I shared what I did. I did painting yesterday in Pinot's palette. | FACTS |

↓

| The Conversation | The Phase |
|---|---|
| Then I asked what he likes to do other than his work. What does he like to read? He shared financial management. I asked for advice. | OPINIONS |

| The Conversation | The Phase |
|---|---|
| Then I asked how is life in the United States. Do they miss family and relatives in India? | FEELINGS |

| The Conversation | The Phase |
|---|---|
| He gave me advice that I should look for girls through my relatives. I agreed and also shared my opinion. Then I shared my feeling that being single is hard. | OPINIONS AND FEELINGS |

## Key Points for Chapter 8

- We think about ourselves a lot
- Become a detective
- Uncover opinions and feelings
- Be curious, and ask what comes to mind

# Chapter 9:
# Build Instant Rapport

IN THIS CHAPTER, you're going to learn how to build instant rapport. Sometimes you only have a few minutes to connect with someone, so I'll show you how you can build rapport quickly with anyone you meet. This is cool stuff, so get excited!

## Rapport Is When People Understand Each Other

Rapport is when two people understand each other. It's that feeling of "Hey, this person gets me." And it doesn't matter how long or even how well you know someone. When you're in rapport, you feel in sync, and you feel like they understand you. You may have experienced this before when you instantly felt close with someone, like you've known them for years, but you couldn't really explain why.

For most people, this usually happens on an unconscious level. They meet someone, and they really like them, but they can't explain why. In this chapter, I'm going to break down that process for you so that you can build rapport with anyone whenever you want.

## We Like People Who Are Like Us

The key thing to understand here is that we like people who are like us. I'll say it again. We like people who are like us. In general, people like other people who are like them. It's natural, and it's even been proven in scientific studies. People are more likely to buy from a salesman who is like them[15] and will even stand closer to people who are like them. The crazy part is the similarity can be anything—age, religion, hobbies, or even food preferences.[16] Any similarity draws people together.

And no matter how small or silly those similarities may seem, it's powerful stuff. For example, this one time I was having dinner, and the waiter was talking about how much he loved peanut butter. I excitedly said, "Me too!" We high-fived and created instant rapport. Boom.

---

15  Sanjaya S. Gaur, Halimin Herjanto, and Hanoku Bathula, "Does Buyer-Seller Similarity Affect Buyer Satisfaction with the Seller Firm?," *International Review of Retail, Distribution and Consumer Research* 22, no. 3 (2012): 315–35, https://doi.org/10.1080/095939 69.2012.682597.

16  Kaitlin Woolley and Ayelet Fishbach, "A Recipe for Friendship: Similar Food Consumption Promotes Trust and Cooperation," *Journal of Consumer Psychology* 27, no. 1 (January 2017): 1–10, https://doi.org/10.1016/j.jcps.2016.06.003.

# Highlight Similarities to Build Rapport

So in order to build rapport, we have to highlight these similarities. I used to think being passionate and interesting is what made people likable, but that's not true. The truth is, people won't care how interesting you are unless you learn how to relate to them and, in a sense, "become like them."

I'm not saying you change yourself to please other people (never do that). But it's a shift in how you think. There's two ways you can look at people. You could look at the differences, or you could look at the similarities.

There will always be differences between you and other people, but at the same time, there are always similarities. Focus on those similarities, and highlight them. Because that, my friend, is how we build rapport. People connect when they both feel like the other person gets them and thinks what they think or feels what they feel. The most likable people I know basically do this automatically.

# Matching Highlights Similarity

So to build rapport, you need to highlight similarity.

And the best way to do it is by matching the other person. It's also known as "mirroring and matching." Have you noticed that good friends tend to act and even talk alike when they're together? Research has shown that matching—which is basically copying others' body language and words—builds trust and rapport. It works in the subconscious to make people feel comfortable with you.

It instantly creates similarity, and it's the most powerful and natural way to build rapport. Here's how you can do it.

## Affirm What They Say

Simply affirm what they say.

When people share something with you (like their opinions and feelings—see chapter 8), they're putting a piece of themselves out there and seeing how you react. It's a little glimpse of who they are. So you need to show that you "get it." That you understand them.

You can show this by affirming what they say. Here are some easy phrases you can use:

- "Yes."
- "That's true."
- "Tell me about it."
- "I know, right?"
- "Seriously."
- "That makes two of us."

These are just examples, so figure out what works for you. The best approach I've found, and the mother of them all, is "yes, and." Go back to chapter 7 to review this technique. The general rule here is to accept what the other person says with "yes" and then build upon it with "and."

## Talk Like Them

Another way to affirm is to match how they talk. Are they talking really fast and energetically, or are they talking slow and super chill? Are they loud, or are they soft-spoken?

When you match someone's pace/pitch/volume, you automatically match their energy level and meet them where they are. Think about it. If you're tired, there's nothing more annoying than an excited person. And if you're excited, there's nothing more annoying than a tired, low-energy person. So match their energy levels by matching how they talk.

You can also talk like them by using their words. It's super powerful. Great communicators do this a lot. Basically, you repeat the person's words back to them. In psychology, it's called the "echo effect." And what it does is show that you get it, and it makes people like you and trust you.

So, for example, at work the other day, I helped my coworker, and she thanked me: "I should always come to you for help." And I simply replied with "always." Instead of trying to come up with a clever response, I just echoed her words back at her. She laughed, and it was cool. I could've said something like "most certainly" or "you got it," but there's something really powerful about reflecting someone's own words back at them.

Try it out, and you'll be surprised how well this works.

## Move Like Them

And lastly, to affirm someone, you can move like them. When two people are in rapport, they actually start moving like each other. But what we can do is match someone's body language on purpose and create that state of rapport. This sends unconscious signals to the person that you're similar to them. Think of it as matching their vibe.

So, for example, when you meet people who are standing up straight with their chest out, stand up a little straighter. If they're relaxed and slouched over, relax your posture too. If they lean in when they're talking, lean in a little bit. If they're breathing slowly, you breathe slowly. If they tilt their head, tilt yours a little.

Remember, you're not copying everything they do. Instead, think of it as getting in sync with their physiology. When people's bodies match, their minds also match. I've found that, for example, when people are walking together, you can tell if their moods match if their footsteps match.

In summary, to build rapport you need to highlight similarity. The best way to do this is by affirming them, talking like them and moving like them.

# Key Points for Chapter 9

- Rapport is when people understand each other
- We like people who are like us
- Highlight similarities to build rapport
- Matching highlights similarity
- Affirm what they say
- Talk like them and move like them

# Step Three: Make a Lasting Impression

# Chapter 10:
# Have Awesome Responses

IN THIS CHAPTER, you'll learn how to have awesome responses. How you respond will determine the impression you leave on someone. I'll explain how this works and give you a simple fill-in-the-blank formula to use.

## Don't Be Like This Guy

I have a friend named Alex. This one time, we were having lunch together. It was a beautiful Sunday afternoon and there was a woman next to us whom he started talking to. I noticed he kept responding with "That's so cool" after everything she said:

WOMAN.  My daughter's in college.
ALEX.   That's so cool.
WOMAN.  She's actually in Africa right now.
ALEX.   That's so cool.
WOMAN.  And she's studying endangered bird species.
ALEX.   Wow. That's so cool.

Now what happened was Alex got to know a lot about the woman and her daughter who studies birds in Africa. But the woman didn't get to know Alex at all—except that he thought everything she was saying was cool. I mean, the conversation wasn't bad, and I'm sure the lady enjoyed it, but did she walk away with a strong impression of Alex? Nope. This is why how you respond is so important.

## Relate to What They Say

To leave an impression, you need to relate to what they're saying. If that's not happening, it's not a conversation (it's a monologue). So what we want to do is leave an impression by relating. When you relate to what they're saying, they remember you as someone they connected with.

In chapters 8 and 9, we learned how to uncover opinions and feelings and match them. Now we can't just go on matching everything they say because that's weird. You need to share your opinions and your feeling as well! And you do that by relating to what they say. Remember this graph below?

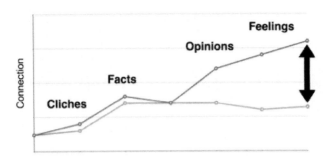

Imagine the darker line represents the other person. Notice how they've moved along to opinions and feelings. Now imagine the lighter line represents you. Notice how you've stayed at the facts level. See the big gap between you and the other person?

That's what happens if you don't share your own opinions and feelings. The other person's opening up, and you're stuck in facts. There's a disconnect.

For true connection to happen, both people have to share.

And the lines should look more like this:

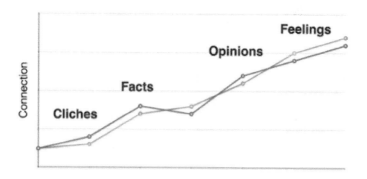

This is why having responses is important. After all, you can't just keep affirming people. They won't connect with you unless you share about yourself too. And the best way to do so? Show how you're similar by relating to what they say.

## Share Your Opinions and Feelings

You don't have to be clever—all you have to do is

relate to what they're saying. OK, so how do you do that? Here's a simple fill-in-the-blank formula: "That's so ____ because ____."

Just insert your opinions and feelings in the blanks. Doesn't get easier than that. So here are some things Alex could have said instead:

- "That's so cool because birds are such fascinating creatures."
- "That's so cool because I've never heard of people doing that."
- "That's so cool. I've always wanted to go to Africa."

Feel free to replace the word *cool* with whatever you like:

- "That's so great."
- "That's so interesting."
- "That's so exciting."
- "That's so funny."

The key is to keep it positive.

## You Can Relate to Anything

Let me show you how easy this is. I want you to think about cookies. Now off the bat, cookies aren't very interesting. They're just a simple, everyday object. We'd categorize this as a "fact" on our graph. But take a second to really think about cookies and connect with some memories you have about cookies.

What are some things that come to mind? What are some opinions? Do any feelings arise?

For me, I love a classic chocolate chip cookie. In my opinion, it's the king of all cookies. Nothing beats chocolate chip—especially if it's crispy on the edges and warm and gooey on the inside. That's the best. And even better, if you eat it with a scoop of vanilla ice cream...oh man, it's so good. It totally reminds me of my childhood.

Do you see how I took cookies and connected it to my own experiences and opinions? You can do that with any topic—even things you know nothing about. Let's do another example and see how this works in conversation.

Let's say you're talking to someone whom you discover is an avid runner. They start talking about how they love running. Here's how you can relate.

Option one: If you *can* relate to running, that's great! Simply use the equation. So, for example, you might say something like the following:

- "That's so *awesome* because *I used to run track*."

- "That's so *funny* because *my best friend just ran a marathon*."

- "That's *such a coincidence* because *I just watched the Usain Bolt documentary*."

Whatever. However you can relate to it. "That's so _____ because _____." Easy, right? And then if you want to keep it going, simply ask a follow-up question, like "How did you get into running?" or "How long have you been running?" or "Do you run races?"

Option two: Now what happens if you *can't* relate *at all* to what they're talking about, and nothing comes to mind? How do you connect and show similarity? What you're going to do is move along the connection line again and relate on an emotional level. So move on to feelings.

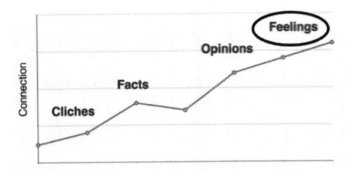

You won't always have the same interests and opinions, and that's fine. So what you can do is relate to their feelings. Connect with their excitement and get excited about the topic with them.

So, for example...

- They're really excited about hiking, but you're not. Take that energy and talk about something related, like nature or exercise.

- They love *Lord of the Rings*, and you know nothing about it. Again, take that energy and talk about something related, like other fantasy movies or movies in general.

The point is, you can to relate to what they say whether you can relate to the topic or not. Conversations need to go back and forth, and ideas need to go both ways. You can start by using the "That's so _____ because _____" equation.

---

## Key Points for Chapter 10

- Relate to what they say
- Share your opinions and feelings
- You can relate to anything

# Chapter 11:
# Exit Gracefully

THE LAST STEP is all about how you exit the conversation. I'm going to show you how to do it gracefully so that people remember you. This technique is so good that you'll actually get stuck in someone's head until the next time they talk to you.

## Last Impressions Are Lasting Impressions

We hear a lot about first impressions and how important they are. But almost nobody talks about last impressions. Last impressions are more powerful than first impressions. Last impressions are what people remember about you. It's how they feel after they talk to you, and it's what makes them look forward to talking to you again.

And a big part of creating that last impression is how you exit the conversation. It can be tricky because we don't want to be rude or awkward. So I'll teach you the absolute best way to exit.

But first you must understand the anatomy of a conversation. This hill in the figure below represents a conversation. Specifically, the up and down represent the rise and fall of the energy level.

**This hill is a conversation.**

The left side is where the conversation starts. The energy increases as people move to the right, as they build rapport. But at some point, and this is true for any conversation—it could be two minutes or two hours—the conversation will start to slow down, and the energy will start to decrease. It's completely normal, and that's what happens.

But here's the thing. *When* you exit a conversation makes a huge difference. Most people wait for the energy to die and then exit. But then it's awkward, and you leave a weird last impression. Instead, what you'll do is exit on a high note, when the energy is high. What this does is it leaves an awesome impression of you in someone's mind.

Why does this work? Because of something called the Zeigarnik effect. Bluma Zeigarnik was a Russian psychologist, and she discovered something amazing about our brains. But I'll get back to that later. First, let's show you exactly how you can do it. The graceful exit has three steps.

## Step One: Touch Interrupt

The first thing you want to do is use the touch interrupt. You're going to briefly touch them on the arm or shoulder, for no more than two seconds. This serves two purposes. First, because you're entering their personal space, it creates a pause. This is really useful for people who talk a lot and don't give you a good opportunity to interrupt.

The second thing it does is create a bonding effect. When you touch someone, they'll feel more connected to you, especially if it's during a high point, which is exactly when you're leaving.

## Step Two: Leave Regretfully

OK. Now that you've got their attention, the next step is to leave regretfully. What you're going to do here is put the blame on yourself because you need to go do something. When you leave regretfully, it shows that you've enjoyed the conversation, and it also protects their ego. It's not that you don't want to talk to them anymore. It's because there's something you have to do.

Here are a few examples of what you can say:

- "I need to go talk to…"

- "I'm going to go take care of…"
- "I have to …"
- "I promised myself I would…"
- "I want to take a look at…"

The most important thing here is that you don't lie! Be honest about what you're going to do, and then go do it.

## Step Three: End with an Unfinished Thought

The last step is to end with an unfinished thought. So, for example, say something like the following:

- "Oh yeah, remind me to tell you about…, which I think you'll love."
- "There's something really interesting I noticed about you—I'll tell you later!"

You'll interrupt the conversation at a high point using touch, leave regretfully, and then end with an unfinished thought. What this does is burn a positive impression of you into the person's mind, and they'll continue to be reminded of you until they talk to you again. This is the power of the Zeigarnik effect.

# People Remember Incomplete Things

The Zeigarnik effect is basically this: people remember incomplete things better than completed things. Bluma Zeigarnik discovered this when she was eating at a restaurant and noticed that the waiters had incredible memory for complicated orders, but then once the orders were delivered, the memory was instantly gone.

For whatever reason, when a task is incomplete, our brains will hold onto it until it's finished. It's probably some safety feature built into our brains so we don't forget important stuff.

The television industry has been using this trick for decades to keep people tuning in week after week. On a season finale of my favorite show, *Breaking Bad*, Jesse Pinkman (a drug dealer) is pointing a gun at Gale Boetticher (a scientist). He must kill Gale, even though he doesn't want to. The gun is shaking, and tears are welling in his eyes. "You don't have to do this," begs Gale. *Bang!* The screen flashes white and then fades to black.

Oh my goodness! Did Jesse shoot Gale? Maybe he missed. What happened?

That tension we feel is the Zeigarnik effect. It bugs us and stays in the back of our minds until we get an answer. And that's why the graceful exit works. If we leave something unfinished at the high point of a conversation, it hooks people and burns you into their memory.

So, in summary, during small talk, use the following at the high point of the conversation:

1. Touch interrupt.
2. Leave regretfully.
3. End with an unfinished thought.

Easy enough, right? Go try it out and give it a shot.

---

## Key Points for Chapter 11

- Last impressions are lasting impressions
- First, use the touch interrupt
- Then leave regretfully
- Finally, end with an unfinished thought

# Bonus: Avoid Awkward Silences

# Chapter 12:
# Master Conversation Threading

WELCOME TO THE bonus section! In this chapter, you'll learn a simple way to never run out of things to say, called "conversation threading." If you blank out in conversations, this will help you avoid those awkward silences.

## Threads Are Information That Interest You

Here's the basic concept for conversation threading. When you're talking to someone, a thread is a piece of information that interests you. It can be a

- word,
- topic, or
- idea.

During a conversation, there will be dozens of

threads. Listen very carefully because every word is a potential thread. Threading is then simply pulling on a thread using a statement or a question. As someone talks, you listen for little bits of information (or threads) that interest you and then use that information to continue the conversation.

For example, let's say someone says, "Today I went to the park with my dog."

That seems like a basic sentence, but there's a ton of information here. In these nine words, there are three threads that you can pull. And each of these opens up a whole new line of conversation.

You could talk about **today**:
- "Today's the perfect day for the park."
- "You have any other plans for today?"

You could talk about **parks**:
- "Which park did you go to?"
- "I went to Yosemite last year."

Or you could talk about **dogs**:
- "What kind of dog do you have?"
- "Dogs are the best."
- "That show *Dog Whisperer* is great."

Pick whichever one sparks something in your

mind. What this does is create natural transitions from one topic to another. A lot of people are so worried about what to say that they miss all these threads, which are key for a flowing conversation. So at this point, you may be thinking that all this sounds messy. Isn't jumping from topic to topic awkward? Can you really just pick a random thread and talk about it?

The beauty is that you can really say anything because even if it seems random, as long as it's related to one of the threads, it's natural, and it keeps the conversation flowing.

When you use threading, conversations can take on a life of their own. And this is why threading is great. You don't need to prepare stories. You don't need to worry about what you're going to say next. You just listen, find threads, respond, then repeat. It's simple and supereffective.

## Key Points for Chapter 12

- Threads are information that interest you
- Listen for threads to continue the conversation
- Pull on a thread using a statement or a question
- Threads are key for flowing conversation

# Chapter 13:
# Create Inside Jokes

LET'S TALK ABOUT the callback. This is a technique I absolutely love. It's so easy to do. But I'm telling you, it's going to take your social skills to the next level. In this chapter, I'll show you how to do it and why it's so amazing.

In chapter 12, we already talked about threading and how to use that to keep your conversations going. You listen for threads, pick a thread, pull on it, etc. But if you get stuck, the callback is another great technique to avoid awkward silences. The reason I love it so much is that it's a two for one:

- On one hand, you keep the conversation going.
- On the other hand, it also builds rapport at the same time.

Here's how you do it.

# Revisit a Previous Topic in Different Context

You revisit or "call back" a previous topic in different context. So, after you've talked about a topic and moved on, bring it up again later. But this time, relate it to a new topic, or, in other words, in a different context.

If you have ever watched stand-up comedy, comedians use callbacks all the time, and what this does is create a sense of *familiarity*. When a comedian repeats a joke, for some reason, even if the joke wasn't that funny the first time, somehow it's funnier the second time around. Because it's familiar, you'll notice the audience actually laughs harder. It's like creating that inside joke with an old buddy. Every time you see each other, you can bring up the same story or same joke, and it doesn't get old. It actually strengthens your bond by creating a history of familiarity.

Now with small talk, we can create that same effect using the callback. All you do is pick a topic (seriously, any topic) and mentally hold it in your back pocket. Then when the chance comes up, relate it to a new topic. Bam. Instant inside joke.

Remember, you can seriously use anything as a callback. The callback is really easy and really powerful. Because a callback feels familiar, that's what makes people laugh and feel connected. And throughout the whole conversation, you can even use the same callback to create a continuous thread.

It is so awesome and so easy to use. Give it a shot! (For more details and a link to a video breakdown, go to the "Thirty-Day Small-Talk-Mastery Plan" at the end of the book and check out Day Twenty-Nine.)

## Key Points for Chapter 13

- Use the callback to create inside jokes
- Revisit a previous topic in different context
- Remember, you can use anything as a callback

# Chapter 14:
# Talk about Yourself

A BIG PART of avoiding awkward silences is being able to talk about yourself. A lot of people struggle with this because they feel like their lives are boring and they have nothing to share. But that is simply not true! I know talking about yourself can seem daunting. Don't worry. In this chapter, I'll teach you how to talk about yourself in a way that connects with others.

## Share Your Opinion

The biggest mistake is not expressing our opinion. Instead we say things like "It was OK" or "I don't know." Sharing is important for connecting with people. And the problem is, nobody connects with "It was OK." Nobody connects with "I don't know." Share your opinions, or there's nothing that people can connect with. Even if your opinion is "I don't really care about it," that's better than not sharing!

I know it can be scary, and you don't want to be judged. But if you don't share, it keeps people from connecting with you. Sharing opinions allows people to feel like they know you and to remember you. if you don't have an opinion, you'll be lost in the noise. A key thing is not being threatened by different opinions; it's just a normal part of conversation.

## Figure Out What You Like

It might take some time if you're used to keeping your opinions to yourself, but a good place to start is to think about some simple stuff. Sit down with a piece of paper and make two columns, "likes" and "dislikes," and just list out things you like and things you don't like.

What foods, what kind of music, what type of people, hobbies, and activities? The first step is figuring out what you like. Take five minutes to do this.

## Use Emotional Words

Similar to sharing opinions, sharing emotions helps people get to know you and connect with you. When you talk about yourself, make sure to use more emotional words. That means instead of saying neutral and plain facts, share how you feel about stuff. It doesn't have to be complicated or hard. Add emotional words when you're describing things.

For example, let's say someone asks you what you ate. Instead of saying, "I had the burger," say, "I *loved* the burger; it's the best thing I've had all week." Do you see how that allows people to connect with you more?

## Give a Little More Detail

Also, along the same lines, instead of just giving the plain facts, give a little more detail. If someone asks you, "Where do you work?" instead of saying, "At a marketing company," say, "At a small marketing agency in the city. I figure out how to sell underwear to men." When you give a little more detail, you give the other person threads (see chapter 13).

## Tell Ministories

And finally, talk about yourself by telling a ministory—no need for dramatic, drawn-out stories. Short ministories can work wonders. These are great because they take people on a journey with you. Think of a movie you love. You know the characters, you understand them, and you see their progress. Stories give people a look into who you are and allow them to see what you see.

And there's a universal structure for these stories. They consist of a beginning, middle, and end. The three parts are:

1. setup,
2. conflict, and
3. resolution.

All three parts create what's called a story arc. And every time you tell a story, this is the basic structure you'll follow. And this is all you're going to do.

First, start with the **setup**. This is the hook that gets people's attention. It will be the key information people need to know to appreciate the rest of the story—just the key background stuff. Make sure it's brief and concise. Some people even do this in one sentence.

Then the **conflict**. Introduce the conflict very early on. Every story needs a conflict. And it's also important to tell this ASAP because it lets people know why they should care and listen to the rest of the story. A conflict is something like good versus evil, man versus nature, man versus himself. It can be anything— even something silly like me versus new restaurant.

End with the **resolution**. Every story needs an ending. The resolution lets people have closure. It's an ending to the conflict and gives the story a purpose. It doesn't have to be a happy ending or funny ending, but it does need an ending. Ask yourself, what's the main point I want to convey?

Here's a really simple example:

1. Setup: "So I tried a new sushi place yesterday..."

2. Conflict: "And I found a cockroach under the bed of rice."

3. Resolution: "Don't go to this restaurant!"

Nothing crazy or complicated, just a simple structure that allows you to tell ministories. Of course, your stories can be longer than three sentences, but just think of the primary message you want to convey and use that to fill in the details.

## Key Points for Chapter 14

- Share your opinion
- Figure out what you like
- Use emotional words
- Give a little more detail
- Tell ministories

# Summary

# Chapter 15:
# Bringing It All Together

I HOPE THIS book has opened your eyes and changed the way you see small talk. Small talk is a great way to create opportunities in your life. With one conversation at a time, we can make more friends and create a nicer world. So let's stop throwing small talk to the wind and reclaim it for what it is—the gateway to all relationships.

You're on your way to becoming a small talk master. Here's a quick summary of the key points you've learned:

- **Bonding over information.** Small talk is a social activity that uses your social brain. So remember, it's about bonding and not about information. Don't get caught up analyzing or taking things too literally. We use it as a low-pressure way to get to know other people. It's the path that leads to deeper stuff.

- **Get out of your head.** This is a huge one. Too often, shy people focus on themselves.

Is this weird? Am I being awkward? What do they think of me? What if they don't want to talk to me? Shift your thinking off yourself and onto the other person. Focus on the other people. Instead of thinking, "How am I doing?" focus on them and "How are they doing?"

- **Cliché is OK.** When you're starting a conversation, you don't have to be clever. You don't have to be unique. Just start with something easy. The four ways I've taught you are very easy, simple, and nearly foolproof.

- **Highlight similarity.** People like people who are like themselves. So in order to connect, you highlight similarity. First, uncover opinions and feelings. Then affirm what they say. Then lastly, share your opinions and feelings. You don't have to agree with everything they say, but it's about showing how you relate.

Those are the key, high-level things for you to keep in mind. Now here's a more detailed, step-by-step summary that you can use like an instruction manual. Think of it as your cheat sheet for small talk. There are three simple steps:

1. Start a conversation
2. Connect
3. Leave an impression

**1. Start a conversation.** To start a conversation, use one of these four easy openers: (1) make an observation of a shared experience, (2) give a compliment and ask a question, (3) offer help, or (4) ask the person's opinion. Keep it simple because cliché is OK. And remember to focus on creating comfort by making the other person feel good and being nonthreatening.

**2. Connect.** Next, turn on detective mode. Be curious, and ask what comes to mind. This will move you through the four phases: clichés to facts to opinions to feelings.

- Focus on uncovering opinions and feelings. In other words, move from *what* to *why*. Ask specific questions to get specific answers and move you away from clichés and facts into the deeper stuff.

- Affirm what they say by matching and highlighting similarity.

**3. Leave an impression.**

a. Relate with your opinions and feelings.

b. Use the formula "That's so _____ because _____."

c. Finally, exit during a high note of the conversation—for example, in the middle of laughter. Briefly touch them on the arm or shoulder for about two to three seconds. Leave regretfully by being honest about what you need to go do. End with an unfinished thought to leave them wanting more.

And that's it. It's easy. Anybody can do it. And if you *really* want to simplify, remember these three steps. In any conversation, these are the steps that repeat over and over again. Think of these as the building blocks that build a conversation:

1. Uncover their opinions and feelings.

2. Affirm what they say.

3. Share your opinions and feelings.

I recommend you come back to this chapter daily for the next thirty days. Review it before and after every conversation. Study it until it becomes ingrained in your subconscious. You can download and print out a one-page cheat sheet from www.thefriendformula.com/cheatsheet.

With a little ambition and sense of adventure, you'll be on your way to building an amazing new life full of possibility!

# Thirty-Day Small-Talk-Mastery Plan

# Introduction

I KNOW WE'VE covered a lot of information in this book. The "Thirty-Day Small-Talk-Mastery Plan" is a simple, easy-to-follow guide to connecting with anyone using small talk. It's designed to level up your skills over the next thirty days, whether you're a complete novice or somewhat proficient.

Like any skill, it requires practice, practice, and practice. By following the daily exercises, you can be confident you're building up the key mind-sets and skills you need. Before you know it, you'll be a small talk master—connecting with anyone you meet. The beauty is that small talk is so simple, it's completely possible for anyone to master. And each day this plan will bring you one step closer. Are you excited? Let's do it!

- **Objective:** Easily approach and connect with anyone you meet.

- **Who it's for:** People who want to build more meaningful relationships.

- **What you'll need:** Dedication and willingness to take action.

- **How to do it**: Set aside thirty minutes a day to read the guide and complete the suggested exercises. If you miss a day, it's OK; simply pick up where you left off.

# Guidelines

THE "THIRTY-DAY SMALL-TALK-MASTERY Plan" maps out your tasks for each day. We'll take it one step at a time, building from the ground up and taking small steps that build upon the last. You'll be 100 percent immersed for the next thirty days, focused on honing this secret skill. Simply follow along and enjoy the ride.

To get the most out of it, be sure to take consistent action each and *every* day. You'll learn through simple and practical exercises, both at home and outside. Some exercises will be harder than others, but that's OK. Keep trying and making progress—no matter how small it seems. Each day, you'll grow a little more and bring these pages into your real life.

If you miss a day, don't sweat it, and continue the next day. If you get stuck on an exercise and don't feel comfortable moving forward, that's OK too. Repeat that exercise a few days until you feel comfortable moving on.

The important thing is to continue taking *consistent* and *daily* action while staying focused on your goal. As Robert Collier said, "Success is the sum of small efforts, repeated day in and day out."

## Your Month at a Glance

Below is a snapshot of your month in a thirty-day calendar—a map that tells you *what* you're doing and *how*. Print this out and post in on your wall. Look at it daily. This will remind you of your progress and keep you inspired.

You can download a PDF version at www.thefriendformula.com/30dayplan.

> *The secret to getting ahead is getting started. The secret of getting started is breaking your complex overwhelming tasks into small manageable tasks, and then starting on the first one.*
> —*Mark Twain*

Your next thirty days are organized into three phases:

1. **Motivation.** Days one through three will focus entirely on motivation. Think of this as the gas that fuels your car. Without proper fuel, your car won't run very far.

2. **Mind-set.** Days four through six will focus on mind-set. This is important, so these exercises will be repeated throughout the thirty days. But in the beginning, it's important to focus on

## Your Thirty-Day Plan

| Day 1 | Day 2 | Day 3 | Day 4 | Day 5 | Day 6 | Day 7 |
|---|---|---|---|---|---|---|
| Motivation (vision) | Motivation (purpose) | Motivation (faith) | Mind-set (equalize) | Mind-set (lower filter) | Mind-set (help others) | Start (say hi) |
| **Day 8** | **Day 9** | **Day 10** | **Day 11** | **Day 12** | **Day 13** | **Day 14** |
| Start (ask question) | Start (observation) | Start (compliment and question) | Start (offer help) | Start (ask opinion) | Start (pick your own) | Connect (detective mode) |
| **Day 15** | **Day 16** | **Day 17** | **Day 18** | **Day 19** | **Day 20** | **Day 21** |
| Connect (uncover facts) | Connect (uncover opinions) | Connect (uncover feelings) | Connect ("yes, and") | Connect (talk like them) | Connect (use their words) | Connect (move like them) |
| **Day 22** | **Day 23** | **Day 24** | **Day 25** | **Day 26** | **Day 27** | **Day 28** |
| Impress (monologue game) | Impress (relate) | Impress (share opinions) | Impress (share feelings) | Impress (ministories) | Impress (graceful exit) | Free play (threading) |
| **Day 29** | **Day 30** | | | | | |
| Free play (callback) | Free play (have fun) | | | | | |

getting your mind-set right. These will set the stage for every conversation you have.

3. **Practice**. Days seven through thirty will focus on practice, practice, practice. We break this down into the three steps you learned in the book: starting a conversation, connecting with someone, then leaving an impression.

You may have noticed in the calendar there are two items each day. The first item is the objective, or the "what." This is simply the purpose of the day. The second item (in parentheses) is the exercise, or the "how." This is how you will actually accomplish it.

Take day one as an example:

- "Motivation" is the "what" for day one— focus on building your motivation.

- "Vision" is the "how" for day one—finding your vision.

Each day is broken down this way, into bite-sized pieces. By completing the exercises each day for the next thirty days, you will absolutely transform your life.

# Day One:
# Motivation—Your Vision

**What:** Build your motivation.
**How:** Find your vision.

WELCOME TO DAY one! Today we start with the most important thing: your motivation. You need strong motivation to keep yourself going. When you feel like giving up, your motivation will push you forward and keep your focused.

The quality of your motivation determines the quality of your results.

To build your motivation, first imagine what you want your future to be. *What* is it that you're working toward? This is your vision. It will serve as your North Star. This is the destination you're headed to. Everything you do will be working toward this goal.

The reason we do this is that anything you want to accomplish must first be formed in your mind as a vision. For example, if you want to bake a cake, you have to envision it first as an idea. If you want to stand up, go outside, and drive to the store, you have to think about those things before they happen. It's no different here.

Let's craft the vision of where you want to be with your small talk:

1. Take out a piece of paper and write down each day of the week across the top: Monday, Tuesday, Wednesday, Thursday, Friday, Saturday, and Sunday.

2. Now, underneath each day, write down all the places that you usually go during those days—anywhere you go. Write it all down (e.g., Monday through Friday, you go to work; you take the bus on Tuesdays and Thursdays; Mondays are for grocery shopping).

3. Next to each place, write down the types of people you see. All the people you see (e.g., at work, it could be your coworkers, bosses, owners, clients, or even the cleaning staff; at the store, it could be cashiers, butchers, or other shoppers).

4. Look at your list and start imagining what it would be like to make small talk with all those people. Much of this will be based on past experiences, but that's OK; just be honest.

   a. How does it go?

   b. How do people react?

   c. How does it make you feel?

   d. Is it easy or hard?

5. Now it's time to create your vision. Think about your ideal future. Start imagining what it *could* be like or how you'd like it to go. Imagine if you could easily make friends

everywhere you went. Now answer the questions again.

   a. How does it go?

   b. How do people react?

   c. How does it make you feel?

   d. Is it easy or hard?

6. Allow your mind to dwell on this vision. How would your life improve? Work? Public transportation? Even grocery shopping?

7. As often as you can, take a moment to close your eyes and imagine your future vision. Remind yourself that this is what you're working toward.

**Optional reading:** For reference, refer to chapter 1, "The Purpose of Small Talk."

# Day Two:
# Motivation—Your Purpose

**What:** Build your motivation.
**How:** Find your purpose.

YESTERDAY WE DEVELOPED your vision, the goal you're working toward, which is your destination. Today, we will find your purpose. The driving force behind your motivation—or the reason *why* you push forward. Think of this as the fuel in your car that gives you energy. Without a strong purpose, you won't last very long.

1. Below are the main ideas from chapter 2. Check off the *one* that resonates with you most, or feel free to create your own.

2. Ask yourself: Which helps the most with changing the way I see small talk? Which helps me to be excited? Which do I find most motivating?

   ☐ It strengthens my social "default mode" brain

   ☐ The purpose is bonding over information

   ☐ It's about communicating emotions and not my actual words

   ☐ Everyone I meet is a genius

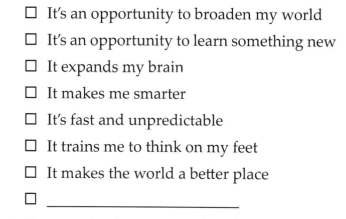

- ☐ It's an opportunity to broaden my world
- ☐ It's an opportunity to learn something new
- ☐ It expands my brain
- ☐ It makes me smarter
- ☐ It's fast and unpredictable
- ☐ It trains me to think on my feet
- ☐ It makes the world a better place
- ☐ _____

3. Once you're done, remember this reason and commit it to memory. Keep it deep in your mind.

4. Now dwell upon your vision from day one, and reinforce it with your purpose. You now know where you're going and why.

Having a purpose is extremely helpful, even in the middle of a conversation. For example, when you find yourself making small talk and you notice your mind is wandering, or you find yourself thinking, "Oh no, I'm getting bored—brain is shutting off," quickly remind yourself of the reason you picked earlier. Use it to inspire you and reinvigorate you. You'll notice that if you give your brain a reason to focus, it'll be much easier to give your full attention to the conversation.

**Optional reading:** For reference, refer to chapter 2, "Small Talk Does Big Things."

# Day Three:
# Motivation—Your Faith

**What:** Build your motivation.
**How:** Develop your faith.

IT CAN BE tempting to give up when the road doesn't look like your destination, when your circumstances don't reflect your vision, when you *know* you're meant to be greater, to do more. But you look around and reality tells you otherwise. This is why we will next develop your faith.

If vision is the destination and purpose is the fuel, then think of faith as your GPS. It gives you confidence that the destination is at hand and will only be a matter of time.

There is no doubt you *will* get there. You know you have what it takes, but you just need *faith*—faith that if you keep on trying, putting in work, you will inevitably arrive.

1.  First, allow your mind to dwell on your vision. What does your life look like? Social life? Family life? Professional life?

2.  Imagine it playing like a movie inside your mind. The more detailed you can envision it, the better.

3. Remind yourself of your purpose while you hold the image in your mind.

4. Next, mentally take hold, enjoy, and feel it, as if you've already arrived at your destination — not with an anxious heart but with a heart of gratitude.

5. Be thankful that you're on this journey, and have *faith* that this path is leading you to your destination.

Faith is about the road you're on, not how far you've come. It's not a matter of success or failure; it's a matter of choosing your destination and sticking with that choice in full faith, until it becomes a reality.

# Day Four:
## Mind-Set—Equalize

**What:** Build your mind-set to stop nervousness.
**How:** Stop comparing, and equalize.

NOW THAT WE have your motivation in place, today we will begin building the proper mind-set. Without the right mind-set, all your attempts at connecting with others will be futile. Your focus will be on all the wrong things.

If you're like me or most people, nervousness is the number one challenge with talking to strangers. Today, we'll focus on an exercise to overcome nervousness. The basic idea is to stop the root cause: comparing. When you compare, it hurts your ability to make small talk and friends. The more you do it, the more nervous you actually become. Here's how you can replace this bad habit with a good one, something I call "equalizing."

1.  Go outside to somewhere public—the more people, the better. A nearby Starbucks, mall, or park bench would be perfect. Anywhere you can sit down and people-watch without looking like a creep.

2.  Now let your thoughts flow as people walk by. Simply observe. Don't force anything, and

don't judge yourself if weird thoughts pop into your head.

3. Begin to notice your thoughts. Notice the way you analyze people and size them up—their clothes, attractiveness, gender, confidence, head size, nose shape...whatever. Become aware of what you notice.

4. After another five minutes, continue to observe, but begin to look for times when you "compare up" (think someone's better than you) or "compare down" (think someone's worse than you). Do you notice the way your mind naturally links back to yourself when you do this? Chances are, these are things you're insecure or prideful about. But moving on...

5. When you notice yourself comparing down, make up something about the person that raises their value. Anything. It doesn't matter if it's true or not, or how ridiculous or random it is. In your mind, create a story, turn that person into a character, and make up some secret talent or special trait that makes them awesome. For example, maybe they're overweight...but an incredibly dedicated parent. Maybe they're homeless...but it's because they donated all their money to orphans.

   f. Having trouble? Go watch this video now: www.thefriendformula.com/equalizeup

g. Notice how people (including yourself) judge and even scoff based on appearance—but how quickly they learn they are wrong. In the same way, when you compare down, use this exercise to remind you that each person has something amazing to share with the world.

6. And if you catch yourself comparing up, do the opposite and make up something that lowers the person's value in your mind. Maybe they're rich…but incredibly lonely. Maybe they're ridiculously good-looking…but they're really dumb and have bad breath. Again, these don't have to be very clever—anything works.

g. Having trouble? Watch this video: www.thefriendformula.com/equalizedown

h. This video is a good reminder that, underneath it all, we are all the same. The beautiful or the rich or the famous are no better than "the rest of us."

Now these are just two silly examples, but the underlying principle is important: people are people. We all have our good, bad, ups, and downs. Stop comparing, and start equalizing!

**Optional reading:** For reference, refer to chapter 3, "Stop Feeling Nervous."

# Day Five:
# Mind-Set—Lower Your Filter

**What:** Build your mind-set to speak freely.

**How:** Lower your filter (bring your thoughts from inside to outside).

YESTERDAY WE COVERED nervousness. Today we'll cover having the right mind-set so that you can speak freely. Remember, without the right mind-set, all your attempts will be futile. And when it comes to speaking freely and not getting stuck with that frozen/speechless feeling, it's *all* about mind-set.

I know what you're thinking: You're not interesting. You don't have much say. But I'm telling you with 100 percent confidence: you are interesting, and you do have something to say. Every person has thoughts, and every person has things worth saying. It's a matter of bringing those ideas from inside to the outside. The way we do this is by lowering our filter.

1.  First, find a private place where nobody will hear you (like your bedroom or your car)—somewhere you're not worried about people hearing you.

2.  Now it's just you and your thoughts. Let your thoughts flow and *say everything* that comes into your mind—literally everything.

3. It's going to feel weird, and you'll notice you filter yourself even though you're alone...but remember, it's just you; nobody can hear you, so say everything you're thinking! What we're doing here is exercising your ability to turn off your filter.

4. Spend at least five minutes doing this every day. At first it will be hard, and you'll hate the sound of your voice, but over time it will get easier, and it'll be easier to just let the words flow.

5. To take it to the next level, record yourself doing this exercise. This is going to make you feel even more self-conscious because now it will feel like someone's listening to you. You can use your phone or computer microphone or whatever you have, and go ahead and record your stream of consciousness for five minutes.

6. If you're brave, go ahead and listen to the recording.

The more you do it, the better you'll get. And over time you'll find you start to trust and even like the sound of your own voice. And in some situations, it may actually be more difficult *not* to speak up.

**Optional reading:** For reference, refer to chapter 5, "Become a Natural."

# Day Six:
# Mind-Set—Help Others

**What:** Build your mind-set to increase social confidence.

**How:** Shift your focus onto others by helping them.

TODAY WE'LL COVER having the right mind-set so that you can build your social confidence. Recall from chapter 4 that true social confidence comes from focusing on others, not yourself. So each time you talk with someone, ask yourself, "How can I leave this person better than when I found them?"

There are thousands of ways you can help others. You can

- make them laugh,
- make them feel listened to,
- compliment their smile,
- let them go ahead of you in line, or
- leave them a generous tip.

Helping others is extremely powerful. It shifts the focus onto others and builds your social confidence. It proves to you, deep down, that you are a good person who knows how to think about others.

**Optional reading:** For reference, refer to chapter 4, "Build True Confidence."

# Day Seven:
## Start—Say Hi

**What:** Start talking to people.
**How:** Say hi to strangers.

**Motivation warm-up:** Start by reminding yourself of your vision, purpose, and faith. Visualize it, feel it, and believe it.

**Mind-set warm-up:** Talk out loud for five minutes (see day five) to lower your filter.

TODAY, WE'LL GET you used to approaching people by simply saying hi. This is where a lot of people get stuck. They think too far ahead, play the scenario out, and end up paralyzed in fear. We're going to smash that fear by taking small action, building small wins, and then building from there.

Saying hi to strangers is easy and fun. The key is doing it without expectation. Here's your task for today. Say hi to ten strangers today. You can find them anywhere. Basically go out anywhere that's not your house.

Now these don't need to be long conversations. Simply say hi. If someone simply says hi back, or you have a five-second conversation, great job. That's one done notch on the belt. And you're one step closer.

Here are a few tips:

- It's helpful to make eye contact before saying hi
- If people aren't making eye contact, you can get their attention by waving—or find people who are standing still
- Use your body. Wave a hand, nod your head, or smile
- Switch it up and throw in a "Have a nice day" or "How are you?"

The point of this exercise is to get used to the idea of approaching new people and making it into a habit. My ultimate goal for you is to get to a point where it almost seems rude if you're not making small talk with people around you.

I know it's scary, but trust me on this one and take the jump. It seems terrifying, but it'll be the most exhilarating thing. Take the leap and start making small talk with new people. It will be one of the most exciting, life-changing things you can do for your life.

# Day Eight:
# Start—Ask a Simple Question

**What:** Start talking to people.
**How:** Ask a simple question.

**Motivation warm-up:** Start by reminding yourself of your vision, purpose, and faith. Visualize it, feel it, and believe it.

**Mind-set warm-up:** Talk out loud for five minutes (see day five) to lower your filter.

OK, SO YOU'VE said hi to a bunch of people by now. If you still don't feel comfortable doing it, go back and repeat day seven over again until you do. By now, you've seen that it's nothing to be scared of. It's easy and fun. And most people are nice.

Today, we're going to kick it up a notch. Here's the plan:

1. Go outside and find a public place with a good flow of people (office, mall, supermarket, downtown, etc.).

2. Start by saying hi to someone.

3. Next, ask them a simple question, ask them for their help—something easy and quick. Here are a few suggestions:

   a. "Hey, do you know what time is it?"

    b. "Can you point me to the nearest bathroom?"

4. Listen for their response, and thank them. That's it!

5. Do this ten times today.

We're taking the conversation to the next level, beyond a simple hi. The focus here is on asking a simple question that asks someone for help. You'll see that 99 percent of people are very willing to do so. People in general are nice, and there's nothing to be afraid of. If anything, you're at an advantage because you have this book and know exactly what you're doing.

Practice asking people simple questions. It's like cracking the door open and peeking inside. It's not scary, and it's great practice. Once you're comfortable, we'll use this forward momentum to keep it going and take it to the next level. For today, just focus on saying hi and then asking a simple question. Easy enough, right? All right, go have fun!

**Optional reading:** For reference, refer to chapter 6, "Easiest Way to Start Talking to Anyone."

# Day Nine:
## Start—Observation

**What:** Start talking to people.

**How:** Make an observation of a shared experience.

**Motivation warm-up:** Start by reminding yourself of your vision, purpose, and faith. Visualize it, feel it, and believe it.

**Mind-set warm-up:** Do the equalizing exercise from day four. Before talking to anyone, sit down and observe people walking by, and equalize them.

TODAY WE MAKE a shift. So far, we've been focusing on *you*—your motivation, your mind-set, getting comfortable approaching people. Today, we're going to start approaching people while focusing on *them*.

We've already gotten warmed up with the equalizing exercise. Now as you approach people, it's important to keep the focus on them—not on what they think of you, what you look like, and especially not on how you feel. The focus is 100 percent on connecting with someone else and understanding where they're at.

So today, you'll start talking to someone with an observation of a shared experience. This will require you to see things from their perspective. Here's how:

    1. Go outside and find a public place with a

good flow of people (office, mall, supermarket, downtown, etc.).

2. Start by asking yourself, "What is everyone here probably feeling right now?" Use that as the spark to start.

3. Look around and make observations about the environment, experience, or people. Specifically, you could comment on

   a. the weather and/or temperature;

   b. décor;

   c. clothing;

   d. food; or

   e. customer service.

4. Here are a few examples from chapter 6:

   a. "Wow, this place is packed."

   b. "Is it just me, or is it insanely hot in here?"

   c. "Did you see that?"

5. Do this five times today.

Remember, your goal is simply to start conversations with people. Don't worry about what happens next. That's not your concern right now. Your only task is to start rolling the ball, and just let it go. The rest will be covered later.

**Optional reading:** For reference, refer to chapter 6, "Easiest Way to Start Talking to Anyone."

# Day Ten:
# Start—Compliment and Question

**What:** Start talking to people.
**How:** Give a compliment, and then ask a question.

**Motivation warm-up:** Start by reminding yourself of your vision, purpose, and faith. Visualize it, feel it, and believe it.
**Mind-set warm-up:** Do the equalizing exercise from day four. Before talking to anyone, sit down and observe people walking by, and equalize them.

THIS OPENER IS very easy and effective. Simply compliment someone, and then ask them a follow-up question. The important thing here is to *quickly* follow the compliment with a question. This keeps the conversation moving forward, as many people don't know how to graciously receive compliments and often get stuck not knowing how to respond.

1. Go outside and find a public place with a good flow of people (office, mall, supermarket, downtown, etc.).
2. Walk around and start saying hi to random people.
3. If something about someone catches your eye, here's your chance to give them a compliment. Here are a few things you can compliment them

on without seeming creepy. In general, try to stay away from appearances and compliment things that they can control. The most important thing is that it be genuine and sincere.

   a. Clothes and accessories (my personal favorite—it's personal but not too personal)

   b. Hairstyle

   c. Something nice or cool they did

   d. Their pet

4. Some people may not know how to react. They may get embarrassed or not know what to say. This is why the next part is so important.

5. Ask a follow-up question. Become curious. Here are some examples:

   a. "I love your hat. Where did you get it?"

   b. "Your haircut is so cool. What's that style called?"

   c. "Wow, your dog is so well trained. How do you do that?"

6. And that's it!

7. Do this a minimum of five times today.

Remember, the important thing is to simply start conversations. It doesn't matter how long they last or what happens afterward. If you start a conversation, consider it a success. We'll master what comes next later.

**Optional reading:** For reference, refer to chapter 6, "Easiest Way to Start Talking to Anyone."

# Day Eleven:
# Start—Offer Help

**What:** Start talking to people.
**How:** Offer to help them.

**Motivation warm-up:** Start by reminding yourself of your vision, purpose, and faith. Visualize it, feel it, and believe it.
**Mind-set warm-up:** Do the equalizing exercise from day four. Before talking to anyone, sit down and observe people walking by, and equalize them.

TODAY'S EXERCISE IS very simple. You will simply go out, look for people who need help, and help them.

I'd like to remind you why this is so great. First of all, it gets you in the right mind-set by focusing on others and expecting nothing in return. Second, it triggers the rule of reciprocity and creates goodwill. Third, helping others has a huge ripple effect on the community.

1.  Go outside and find a public place with a good flow of people (office, mall, supermarket, downtown, etc.).

2.  Walk around and start saying hi to random people.

3. Look for people that need help, and simply help them. Here are a few examples:

   a. Give directions to someone who is lost

   b. Hold a door open

   c. Leave a big tip for your waiter

   d. Help someone carry a heavy item

   e. Pay for someone's order

4. If you strike up a conversation, great. If not, no problem. Move on to help the next person.

5. Do this at least five times today.

Remember, the important thing is to get in the mind-set of helping people and simply start conversations. It doesn't matter how long they last or what happens afterward. If you start a conversation, consider it a success. We'll master what comes next later.

**Optional reading:** For reference, refer to chapter 6, "Easiest Way to Start Talking to Anyone."

# Day Twelve:
## Start—Ask Opinion

**What:** Start talking to people.
**How:** Ask their opinion.

**Motivation warm-up:** Start by reminding yourself of your vision, purpose, and faith. Visualize it, feel it, and believe it.
**Mind-set warm-up:** Do the equalizing exercise from day four. Before talking to anyone, sit down and observe people walking by, and equalize them.

THIS OPENER IS my absolute favorite. It's tons of fun and a great way to start talking to people in a nonthreatening way.

1.  Go run an errand at a store (clothing, grocery, restaurant, etc.)—anywhere you need to make purchase decisions.

2.  As you're browsing or waiting in line, turn to someone next to you and ask for their opinion. Here are some examples:

    a.  "Excuse, can I get your opinion on something?"

    b.  "Which one of these hats looks better on me?"

c. "Have you ever tried their cheesecake? Would you recommend it?"

d. "What's your favorite item on the menu?"

3. This is amazing because it jumps to the opinions stage. In a way, we're hacking the connection curve and skipping the clichés and facts stages (see chapter 8).

4. If you strike up a conversation, great. If not, no problem. Move on to the next person.

5. Do this at least five times today.

Remember, the important thing is to simply start conversations. It doesn't matter how long they last or what happens afterward. If you start a conversation, consider it a success. We'll master what comes next later.

**Optional reading:** For reference, refer to chapter 6, "Easiest Way to Start Talking to Anyone."

# Day Thirteen:
# Start—Pick Your Own

**What:** Start talking to people.

**How:** Pick your own openers.

**Motivation warm-up:** Start by reminding yourself of your vision, purpose, and faith. Visualize it, feel it, and believe it.

**Mind-set warm-up:** Do the equalizing exercise from day four. Before talking to anyone, sit down and observe people walking by, and equalize them.

TODAY YOU'RE GOING to have some freedom to do what you want, to take the lessons and experiences from days seven through twelve and make them your own.

1. Go outside and find a public place with a good flow of people (office, mall, supermarket, downtown, etc.).

2. Walk around and start saying hi to random people.

3. Find someone to talk to.

4. Use any opener that you choose. You can make an observation, compliment, offer help, ask their opinion, or create your own individual approach.

5. The key here is to just have fun!

6. Start conversations with at least five people today.

Remember, the important thing is to simply *start* conversations. It doesn't matter how long they last or what happens afterward. If you start a conversation, consider it a success. We'll master what comes next starting tomorrow.

**Optional reading:** For reference, refer to chapter 6, "Easiest Way to Start Talking to Anyone."

# Day Fourteen:
## Connect—Detective Mode

**What:** Connect with people.
**How:** Turn on detective mode.

**Motivation warm-up:** Start by reminding yourself of your vision, purpose, and faith. Visualize it, feel it, and believe it.

**Mind-set warm-up:** Shift your focus off yourself and onto others. This will decrease your nervousness and open up your curiosity. It may help to ask yourself, "How can I leave this person better than when I found them?"

CONGRATULATIONS ON MAKING it to day fourteen, the second week of the "Thirty-Day Small-Talk-Mastery Plan"! Take a moment right now to pat yourself on the back. You picked up this book, read it, then followed through with the action plan. This puts you in the top percentage of people. Not many have the guts and determination to take action and learn a new skill. You're doing a great job.

Now up until this point, we've been focusing on your mind-set and practicing how to approach people and say hi. Starting conversations (days seven through thirteen) is all about creating that initial opening. For the most part, this is going to require clichés. Take a moment to refresh with the graph below, from chapter 8.

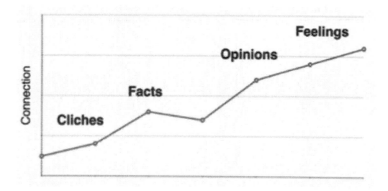

Remember, every conversation consists of these three steps over and over.

1. Uncover their opinions and feelings.

2. Affirm what they say

3. Share your opinions and feelings.

So what we're going to focus on first is step one: uncovering opinions and feelings. OK, let's have some fun. Today, we're going to strengthen your ability to identify types of statements and more importantly notice the deepening transitions.

1. Go to your local coffee shop, or even just flip on the TV, and look for some people having conversations. My favorite is watching late-night talk show interviews. Here are a few you can easily watch online:

   a. *The Late Late Show with James Corden*

   b. *The Tonight Show with Jimmy Fallon*

    c. *Conan*

    d. *The Late Late Show with Craig Ferguson* (It's off the air, but my personal favorite)

2. As you listen, really pay attention; and as people talk, categorize what they say. Are they using clichés? Talking about facts? Discussing opinions? Sharing feelings?

3. Go download and print the worksheet from www.thefriendformula.com/detective.

4. Take notes on the types of things people say as you listen, and put them in their categories.

5. Also notice the transitions between each of these categories.

It'll take a bit of thinking at first, but soon you'll be able to recognize the phases effortlessly and move through them like a conversational ninja.

**Optional reading:** For reference, refer to chapter 8, "Turn on Detective Mode."

# Day Fifteen:
## Connect—Uncover Facts

**What:** Connect with people.
**How:** Turn on detective mode and uncover facts.

**Motivation warm-up:** Start by reminding yourself of your vision, purpose, and faith. Visualize it, feel it, and believe it.
**Mind-set warm-up:** Shift your focus off yourself and onto others.

YESTERDAY YOU OBSERVED people having conversations. You noted the transitions from clichés to facts to opinions to feelings. Today we will practice doing this with people. But don't worry; we'll take it one step at a time.

1. Go outside and find a public place with a good flow of people (office, mall, supermarket, downtown, etc.).

2. Walk around and start saying hi to random people.

3. Start a conversation with someone using one of the four easy openers (see days nine through twelve).

4. Now to bring the conversation forward, turn on detective mode and become curious about

the other person. What is their story? How are they doing? What can you learn from them?

5. Uncover facts about the person's life. Here are some examples:

    a. Where are they from?

    b. How's their day going?

    c. What do they do for work?

    d. What do they do for fun?

    e. Do they have siblings?

    f. Can they speak another language?

    g. How often do they travel?

6. And that's it. Don't worry about connecting or how you end the conversation. We'll cover that later. Simply uncover facts about the other person.

7. Repeat this five times today with five different people.

**Optional reading:** For reference, refer to chapter 8, "Turn on Detective Mode."

# Day Sixteen:
# Connect—Uncover Opinions

**What:** Connect with people.
**How:** Turn on detective mode and uncover opinions.

**Motivation warm-up:** Start by reminding yourself of your vision, purpose, and faith. Visualize it, feel it, and believe it.
**Mind-set warm-up:** Shift your focus off yourself and onto others.

GREAT JOB YESTERDAY uncovering facts. Today, we get to the good stuff: *opinions*! Remember, this transition from facts to opinions is where the magic happens. This is when connections begin to be formed.

So today, we're going to do the same thing as yesterday but focus on transitioning to the next step.

1. Go outside and find a public place with a good flow of people (office, mall, supermarket, downtown, etc.).

2. Walk around and start saying hi to random people.

3. Start a conversation with someone using one of the four easy openers (see days nine through twelve).

4. Now, to bring the conversation forward, turn on detective mode and become curious about the other person.

5. Uncover **facts** about the person's life.

6. As they talk, uncover their **opinions** about certain things. My favorite question to ask is "Do you like...?" Here are some examples:

    a. If they talk about the heat, ask them, "Do you like hot weather?"

    b. If they tell you they live in Phoenix, ask them, "How is Phoenix? Do you like it there?"

7. Uncover one or two opinions, and you're done!

8. Repeat this at least five times today with five different people.

**Optional reading:** For reference, refer to chapter 8, "Turn on Detective Mode."

# Day Seventeen:
## Connect—Uncover Feelings

**What:** Connect with people.
**How:** Turn on detective mode and uncover feelings.

**Motivation warm-up:** Start by reminding yourself of your vision, purpose, and faith. Visualize it, feel it, and believe it.
**Mind-set warm-up:** Shift your focus off yourself and onto others.

GREAT JOB YESTERDAY uncovering opinions. Today, let's move onto feelings. We're going to do the same thing, but this time as we uncover opinions, we're going to look to uncover feelings about those opinions.

1. Go outside and find a public place with a good flow of people (office, mall, supermarket, downtown, etc.).

2. Walk around and start saying hi to random people.

3. Start a conversation with someone using one of the four easy openers (see days nine through twelve).

4. Now to bring the conversation forward, turn on detective mode and become curious about

the other person.

5. Uncover facts about the person's life.

6. As they talk, uncover their opinions about the facts.

7. Now from here, continue to be curious, and ask what comes to mind.

8. The next step is to ask questions that uncover feelings. Here are some examples:

   a. "Do you enjoy that?"

   b. "Are you excited?"

   c. "Does that make you nervous?"

   d. "How amazing does that make you feel?"

9. Uncover one or two feelings, and you're done!

10. Repeat this at least five times today with five different people.

Let's also clarify the difference between opinions and feelings. Think about it like this. Opinions are what people think (eg, preferences, ideas, philosophies, world views, favorite things, etc.). Feelings are what people feel (eg, what makes them sad, angry, excited, etc.).

**Optional reading:** For reference, refer to chapter 8, "Turn on Detective Mode."

# Day Eighteen:
## Connect—"Yes, And"

**What:** Connect with people.
**How:** Affirm what they say.

**Motivation warm-up:** Start by reminding yourself of your vision, purpose, and faith. Visualize it, feel it, and believe it.
**Mind-set warm-up:** Shift your focus off yourself and onto others.

HELLO AGAIN, AND welcome to day eighteen. You're doing a great job. You are now comfortable starting a conversation with anyone and then uncovering their opinions and feelings. Now here's what's next.

Remember that any conversation is a two-way street. We can't just keep asking question after question. That's an interrogation, not a conversation. To be a master of small talk, there are basically three steps that you'll cycle through over and over. These are the fundamental building blocks. So focus on doing these three steps again and again:

1. Uncover their opinions and feelings.
2. Affirm what they say (the focus of today).
3. Share your opinions and feelings.

The focus for today is step two, affirming what the other person says. This is so important in connecting and showing that you hear and understand them. An easy way to get started is by using the "yes, and" rule. It's a great way to create comfort.

First, to see what a big difference this makes, let's take a look at some breakdowns of real conversations. Go to www.thefriendformula.com/awkward and watch the video. This one is really uncomfortable. Notice how many times he says no during this conversation. Pretty terrible, right? Now go to www.thefriendformula.com/yesand and watch the video. This is someone who's mastered the "yes, and" rule. Witness the power of using "yes, and" to create comfort during small talk. Huge difference, right?

Here's the exercise for today:

1. Go outside and find a public place with a good flow of people (office, mall, supermarket, downtown, etc.).

2. Walk around and start saying hi to random people.

3. Start a conversation with someone using one of the four easy openers (see days nine through twelve).

4. Now to bring the conversation forward, turn on detective mode and become curious about the other person.

5. Uncover facts about the person's life.

6. As they talk, uncover their opinions about the facts.

7. Continue to be curious, and uncover their feelings.

8. Next, affirm what people say. Respond by using the "yes, and" method. For a refresher, refer to chapter 9. In general, you want to use phrases that show people you understand them and that you "get it." Examples include the following:

    a. "Yes."

    b. "That's true."

    c. "Tell me about it."

    d. "I know, right?"

    e. "Seriously."

    f. "That makes two of us."

9. Repeat this at least five times today with five different people.

**Optional reading:** For reference, refer to chapter 7, "The Key Principle of Great Small Talk."

# Day Nineteen:
## Connect—Talk Like Them

**What:** Connect with people.
**How:** Match how they talk.

**Motivation warm-up:** Start by reminding yourself of your vision, purpose, and faith. Visualize it, feel it, and believe it.
**Mind-set warm-up:** Find someone who's walking a different pace than you. Change your speed to match. See what happens, and notice how your mood starts to adjust. This is the power of matching.

YESTERDAY WE PRACTICED affirming people using the "yes, and" rule. This is great for step two below.

1.  Uncover their opinions and feelings.

2.  Affirm what they say (the focus of today).

3.  Share your opinions and feelings.

There are many other ways to affirm people, so that's what we're going to do today. This exercise will help you affirm people and build rapport by matching them. Specifically, we'll start with your voice.

1. Look at the table below and pick *one* item to focus on.

| Talk like them |
| --- |
| ☐ Pace |
| ☐ Pitch |
| ☐ Volume |

2. Go outside and find a public place with a good flow of people (office, mall, supermarket, downtown, etc.).

3. Walk around and start saying hi to random people.

4. Start and have a conversation, using what you learned in days seven through eighteen.

5. Focus on matching this one thing as much as possible in your conversations.

   a. For pace, match how quickly (or slowly) they talk and the rhythm of their sentences.

   b. For pitch, match the changes in inflection when they speak. Some people may use more of a singsong pitch ("Hel-looooo!"), while others may maintain a single pitch.

   c. For volume, simply match how loud or softly they speak. How much air do they put behind their words?

6. The key objective here is that we're matching their energy level and creating similarity.

7.  Do this at least five times today with five different people.

And make sure to take your time. Even if you just focus on one thing for each conversation, you are already ahead of the game. Most people don't even think about this stuff.

**Optional reading:** For reference, refer to chapter 9, "Build Instant Rapport."

# Day Twenty:
## Connect—Use Their Words

**What:** Connect with people.
**How:** Match their words.

**Motivation warm-up:** Start by reminding yourself of your vision, purpose, and faith. Visualize it, feel it, and believe it.

**Mind-set warm-up:** Find someone who's walking a different pace than you. Change your speed to match. See what happens, and notice how your mood starts to adjust. This is the power of matching.

YESTERDAY WE PRACTICED affirming people by matching *how* they talk—matching their voice. Today, you'll practice affirming people by using their words.

1. Go outside and find a public place with a good flow of people (office, mall, supermarket, downtown, etc.).

2. Walk around and start saying hi to random people.

3. Start and have a conversation, using what you learned in days seven through eighteen.

4. When someone shares their opinion or feelings, affirm them using their own words:

    a. They say, "Chocolate cake is the <u>best</u>"; you say, "It really is <u>the best</u>."

    b. They say, "I'm so <u>excited</u>!"; you say, "Yes, that's so <u>exciting</u>!"

5. Do this at least five times today with five different people.

**Optional reading:** For reference, refer to chapter 9, "Build Instant Rapport."

# Day Twenty-One:
# Connect—Move Like Them

**What:** Connect with people.
**How:** Match how they move.

**Motivation warm-up:** Start by reminding yourself of your vision, purpose, and faith. Visualize it, feel it, and believe it.

**Mind-set warm-up:** Find someone who's walking a different pace than you. Change your speed to match. See what happens, and notice how your mood starts to adjust. This is the power of matching.

YESTERDAY WE PRACTICED affirming people by matching their words. Today, you'll practice affirming people by matching their body.

1. Look at the table below and pick *one* item to focus on.

| Move like them |
| --- |
| ☐ Posture |
| ☐ Sitting position |
| ☐ Lean |
| ☐ Hand movements |
| ☐ Breathing |
| ☐ Head tilt |

2. Go outside and find a public place with a good flow of people (office, mall, supermarket, downtown, etc.).

3. Walk around and start saying hi to random people.

4. Start and have a conversation, using what you learned in days seven through eighteen.

5. As they talk, pay attention to how they move their body.

6. Focus on matching this one thing as much as possible in your conversations.

   a. If they stand up straight with their chest out, stand up a little straighter

   b. If they're relaxed and slouched over, relax your posture too

   c. If they lean in when they're talking, lean in a little bit

   d. If they're breathing slowly, slow down your breath

   e. If they tilt their head, tilt yours to mirror it

7. Important caution here: don't copy exactly everything they do. This will seem very robotic and unnatural.

8. The main objective is to match the general position of their body so that you can get in sync. When people's bodies match, their minds match too.

9. Do this at least five times today with five different people.

**Optional reading:** For reference, refer to chapter 9, "Build Instant Rapport."

# Day Twenty-Two:
# Impress—Monologue Game

**What:** Leave an impression.
**How:** Play the monologue game.

**Motivation warm-up:** Start by reminding yourself of your vision, purpose, and faith. Visualize it, feel it, and believe it.
**Mind-set warm-up:** Talk out loud for five minutes (see day five) to lower your filter.

LET'S REVIEW. SO far, we've covered steps one and two below.

1. Uncover their opinions and feelings.

2. Affirm what they say.

3. Share your opinions and feelings (focus of today).

Step three can be tough for some people. It takes practice and creativity. Today you're going to learn a game you can play at home to hone this skill of relating to others by sharing your opinions and feelings.

This one is super fun and probably my favorite. You're going to sharpen your skills using late-night TV shows. OK, here's how it works.

1. Go online, using your computer or phone, and find some late-night monologues.

a. Simply go to YouTube and search "monologue" plus "Jimmy Fallon," "Conan O'Brien," "James Corden," etc. Look for the thumbnails where the host is standing in front of a curtain.

2. Here's how monologues are structured. First, there's a setup (usually a fact from recent news) and then a punchline.

3. Start watching the video, and wait for the first setup.

4. Then pause the video and then think about how you'd respond using the "That's so..." equation.

5. Press play and listen to the punchline (and enjoy a good laugh).

6. Continue watching and repeat steps three through five.

7. And then just continue through the entire monologue.

8. Watch each setup and respond with your thoughts using the equation.

9. For an example of what this looks like, go to www.thefriendformula.com/monologue.

This exercise is great because it trains your brain to relate to random topics. Some topics will be harder than others, but that's OK. Just take your time, and go easy on yourself. Whatever you come up with is fine. You don't have to be funny or witty. Just have fun with it.

Remember, what you're doing is forcing your brain to relate to random topics and build interesting connections. Plus you stay on top of current events, which is an awesome bonus!

**Optional reading:** For reference, refer to chapter 10, "Have Awesome Responses."

# Day Twenty-Three:
## Impress—Relate to Them

**What:** Leave an impression.
**How:** Relate.

**Motivation warm-up:** Start by reminding yourself of your vision, purpose, and faith. Visualize it, feel it, and believe it.
**Mind-set warm-up:** Talk out loud for five minutes (see day five) to lower your filter.

WE'RE GOING TO take what you learned yesterday and apply it in the real world.

1. Go outside and find a public place with a good flow of people (office, mall, supermarket, downtown, etc.).

2. Walk around and start saying hi to random people.

3. Start and have a conversation, using what you learned in days seven through eighteen.

4. When people share their opinions and feelings, use the "That's so _____ because _____" formula:

   a. "That's so funny because…"

   b. "That's so cool because…"

   c. "That's such a coincidence because…"

    d.  "That my favorite because…"

5.  Do this at least five times today with five different people.

**Optional reading:** For reference, refer to chapter 10, "Have Awesome Responses."

# Day Twenty-Four:
# Impress—Share Your Opinions

**What:** Leave an impression.
**How:** Share your opinions.

**Motivation warm-up:** Start by reminding yourself of your vision, purpose, and faith. Visualize it, feel it, and believe it.

**Mind-set warm-up:** Talk out loud for five minutes (see day five) to lower your filter.

IF YOU FOUND the last two days challenging, that's normal. It's not easy for many people to openly share their opinions, especially if they think of themselves as being shy. I find that many people don't actually make an effort to even *know* what their opinions are. I'm absolutely positive you have opinions, but you need to make a conscious effort to be aware of what those are so that you can be passionate and express them to others. This is how other people get to connect with us.

Today will be a two-part exercise. First, before you can share your opinions, you must know what they are. Let's find out.

1.  Find a quiet place and sit down by yourself.

2. Get a piece of paper and draw the table below.

| My likes | My dislikes |
|----------|-------------|
|          |             |

3. Think about and list things you like in the left column.

4. Think about and list things you dislike in the right column.

5. Here are some categories to think about:

   a. Food

   b. Music

   c. Personality types

   d. Movies and shows

   e. Activities

   f. Places

6. Very simple but a great place to start.

7. If you're feeling ambitious, go read or watch the news and write down opinions on the major headlines.

Next, bring this fresh awareness of yourself into real conversations:

1. Go outside and find a public place with a good flow of people (office, mall, supermarket, downtown, etc.).

2. Walk around and start saying hi to random people.

3. Start and have a conversation, using what you learned in days seven through eighteen.

4. When people share their opinions and feelings, affirm what they say.

5. Then share your own opinions.

   a. Find a way to relate to what they've shared

   b. Then share your opinion on the topic or on a related topic

6. Do this at least five times today with five different people.

**Optional reading:** For reference, refer to chapter 15, "Talk about Yourself."

# Day Twenty-Five:
# Impress—Share Your Feelings

**What:** Leave an impression.
**How:** Share your feelings.

**Motivation warm-up:** Start by reminding yourself of your vision, purpose, and faith. Visualize it, feel it, and believe it.
**Mind-set warm-up:** Talk out loud for five minutes (see day five) to lower your filter.

YESTERDAY YOU LISTED out your opinions and practiced sharing them with others. Just like opinions, feelings are important for letting people connect with you. Today, let's practice building this into your conversations.

1. Go outside and find a public place with a good flow of people (office, mall, supermarket, downtown, etc.).

2. Walk around and start saying hi to random people.

3. Start and have a conversation, using what you learned in days seven through eighteen.

4. When people share their opinions and feelings, affirm what they say.

5. Then share your own opinions.

6. To incorporate your feelings, simply use more emotional words. Here are some examples:

   a. "I love..."

   b. "I hate..."

   c. "So excited..."

   d. "I'm so anxious about..."

   e. "It pisses me off when..."

7. Less neutral and boring words—more emotional words!

8. Do this at least five times today with five different people.

**Optional reading:** For reference, refer to chapter 15, "Talk about Yourself."

# Day Twenty-Six:
## Impress—Tell Ministories

**What:** Leave an impression.
**How:** Tell ministories.

**Motivation warm-up:** Start by reminding yourself of your vision, purpose, and faith. Visualize it, feel it, and believe it.
**Mind-set warm-up:** Talk out loud for five minutes (see day five) to lower your filter.

BEING ABLE TO tell stories is a great way to leave an impression. Telling stories draws people in. It allows them into your world. It takes a little effort, but it's well worth it. The secret is to pay attention, remember, then retell. Here's how:

1.  Today, focus on being an observer. Notice how you feel. Notice how others feel. Notice what happens around you.

2.  If anything interesting or funny happens, write it down. Writing things down is really important. Carry around a moleskin or use Evernote on your phone. And make sure to include enough details so you can make sense of it later. Here are a few examples from my notebook:

    a. "Kathy ate dinner before going out to control her appetite. Ended up eating two meals."

    b. "Thomas aggressively cutting his birthday cake while everyone watched in horror."

3. At the end of the day, review your notes.

4. Take each one and reorganize using the setup, conflict, resolution structure. Here is an example:

    a. Setup: "So my friend Kathy ate dinner before meeting us at a restaurant…"

    b. Conflict: "She's on a diet and trying to lose weight."

    c. Resolution: "She ended up eating two dinners. Ha ha!"

5. Continue to collect these stories, remember them, and use them when the right time comes!

**Optional reading:** For reference, refer to chapter 15, "Talk about Yourself."

# Day Twenty-Seven:
## Impress—Graceful Exit

**What:** Leave an impression.
**How:** Gracefully exit.

**Motivation warm-up:** Start by reminding yourself of your vision, purpose, and faith. Visualize it, feel it, and believe it.
**Mind-set warm-up:** Talk out loud for five minutes (see day five) to lower your filter.

REMEMBER THAT LAST impressions are lasting impressions. How you end a conversation is even more important than how you start it. Last impressions are what people will remember about you.

1. Go outside and find a public place with a good flow of people (office, mall, supermarket, downtown, etc.).

2. Walk around and start saying hi to random people.

3. Start a conversation with someone using one of the four easy openers (see days nine through twelve).

4. Turn on detective mode and become curious about the other person.

5. Uncover facts about the person's life.

6. Continue to be curious and uncover their opinions and feelings.

7. Affirm what they say.

8. Share your opinions, feelings, and ministories.

9. Repeat steps five through eight as needed.

10. During a high note, touch the person on the arm for two seconds.

11. Leave regretfully and explain you need to go. Here are some examples:

    a. "I need to go talk to…"

    b. "I'm going to go take care of…"

    c. "I promised myself I would…"

12. End with an unfinished thought. Here are some examples:

    a. "Remind me to tell you about…"

    b. "I've got to show you something amazing later."

13. And that's it!

14. Do this at least five times today with five different people.

**Optional reading:** For reference, refer to chapter 11, "Exit Gracefully."

# Day Twenty-Eight:
## Free Play—Threading

**What:** Avoid awkward silence.
**How:** Use conversation threading.

**Motivation warm-up:** Start by reminding yourself of your vision, purpose, and faith. Visualize it, feel it, and believe it.
**Mind-set warm-up:** Talk out loud for five minutes (see day five) to lower your filter.

TODAY YOU'LL PRACTICE the art of conversation threading. This simple technique will keep your conversations going and help you avoid those awkward silences, when your mind goes blank and you don't know what to say.

1.  Go outside and find a public place with a good flow of people (office, mall, supermarket, downtown, etc.).

2.  Walk around and start saying hi to random people.

3.  Start a conversation with someone using one of the four easy openers (see days nine through twelve).

4.  Turn on detective mode and become curious about the other person.

5. As they're talking, listen for a word, topic, or idea that interests you. It can be anything that sparks something in your mind.

6. Take any sentence, and there are a ton of potential threads you can pull on—for example, if someone says, "This <u>town</u> has the <u>best</u> <u>pizza</u> I've <u>ever</u> eaten," you can talk about

   a. what makes a "best pizza,"

   b. different types of pizza,

   c. pizza toppings,

   d. a story or memory you have about pizza,

   e. other places they or you have tried pizza,

   f. the town you're in, or

   g. other places to eat in the town.

7. You can take any of these and continue the conversation without it seeming random because it's connected to the original sentence. It's natural and keeps the conversation going.

8. Practice this in at least five conversations today with five different people.

Want to see it in action? Go to www. thefriendformula.com/threading to watch me break down a real conversation.

**Optional reading:** For reference, refer to chapter 12, "Master Conversation Threading."

# Day Twenty-Nine:
## Free Play—Callback

**What:** Avoid awkward silences.
**How:** Use the callback.

**Motivation warm-up:** Start by reminding yourself of your vision, purpose, and faith. Visualize it, feel it, and believe it.

**Mind-set warm-up:** Talk out loud for five minutes (see day five) to lower your filter.

THE CALLBACK IS an awesome tool for keeping conversations going. And as a bonus, it's a great way to create inside jokes at the same time. It works with one-on-one or group conversations. The basic idea is to revisit, or "call back," a previous topic in a different context.

1. Go outside and find a public place with a good flow of people (office, mall, supermarket, downtown, etc.).

2. Walk around and start saying hi to random people.

3. Start a conversation with someone using one of the four easy openers (see days nine through twelve).

4. During your conversation, similar to threading, look for keywords or ideas that you can hold onto. It can literally be anything. Here are some examples:

   a. They "love sweaters"

   b. They pronounce the word *also* funny

   c. They believe in "love at first sight"

5. When the conversation has moved on to a different topic, revisit the idea again. Here are some examples:

   a. Say, "I bet you could really use a sweater right now"

   b. Use the word *also* in a sentence and pronounce it like them

   c. Say, "It's like love at first sight"

6. It may help for you to see it in action. Go watch the video breakdown here: www.thefriend formula.com/callback.

**Optional reading:** For reference, refer to chapter 14, "Create Inside Jokes."

# Day Thirty:
# Free Play—Have Fun

**What:** Start talking to anyone, connect, and leave a great impression.
**How:** Have fun.

**Motivation warm-up:** Start by reminding yourself of your vision, purpose, and faith. Visualize it, feel it, and believe it.
**Mind-set warm-up:** Talk out loud for five minutes (see day five) to lower your filter.

CONGRATULATIONS! YOU HAVE made it to the *last* day of the "Thirty-Day Small-Talk-Mastery Plan"! You're a rock star! Since it's the last day, let's just have some fun and use everything you've learned. No need to overthink or focus on any one thing. Simply start talking to people and have fun. In case you need it, here's a summary of all the steps you've learned in these thirty days:

1. Go outside and find a public place with a good flow of people (office, mall, supermarket, downtown, etc.).

2. Walk around and start saying hi to random people.

3. Start a conversation with someone using one of the four easy openers (see days nine through twelve).

4. Turn on detective mode and become curious about the other person.

5. Uncover facts about the person's life.

6. Continue to be curious and uncover their opinions and feelings.

7. Affirm what they say.

8. Share your opinions, feelings, and ministories.

9. Repeat steps five through eight as needed.

10. Exit gracefully.

11. Remember to have fun!

12. Talk to as many people as you'd like.

Printed in Great Britain
by Amazon